LIMITLESS HUMANS

How Running Helped Me Live a Meaningful Life

Sukant Suki Singh

ISBN 9780648715306

For my mum,

Thank you for raising me and teaching me some basic life skills like helping others, cooking and to respect women and honour the value of hard work.

I will always miss you.

Contents

Introduction

It all started when I was born in a north Indian city named Varanasi, earlier known as Benares or Kashi. The city is known as the spiritual capital of India, full of temples and colours. My mum grew up in this city, and unfortunately, she passed away just after I turned 12. This was the first set back in my life but eventually it also made me stronger. My father sent me and my brother to boarding school in the hope of a bright future for us.

I started running at the age of 18 years when I was in one of India's elite high schools. Sports was considered a key to student's overall development and I became the athletics captain in school. I also loved goal keeping in a soccer match but running was my first love.

Graduating from school, I started running marathons, and at the age of 30 now I have completed around 22 marathons including some extraordinary ultra marathons.

Running Marathons have now become a part of my life. It teaches me various life lessons and to deal with the challenges of life like stress, anxiety, depression, failure, and loss of loved ones. My mission is to run 100 marathons around the world before I die and inspire people with a message that running helps.

While I am writing this book, I live in Australia and mental health is a very big issue in this country. One in four people is suffering from stress, anxiety and on an average over 3 people commit suicide in this country every day. The mental health among the indigenous people is even worse due to the loss of their land, and their loved ones. By writing this book, I am just trying to create awareness around how big this issue is. I have myself suffered from stress and anxiety in April, 2019 and if I can inspire one soul who has lost hope to live a meaningful life, then it would be worth running marathons.

In this book, I have laid out the lessons, I learnt while running various marathons and ultra marathons in India and Australia and how it helped me live a more conscious and joyful life. I have also expressed my love for media, film and journalism and talked about my other hobbies like painting and cooking. Painting and cooking have helped me de-stress and live a life with purpose. I describe my journey of running which has helped me make meaningful human connections in the age of technology. I am just trying to connect the dots using all my skills into this book. I ran several marathons by myself and running 100km at the Surf Coast Century was the toughest experience so far.

This book also contains the interviews I conducted while running marathons, I came across some extraordinary runners, people on the planet and their stories. I found my purpose in doing what I love the most, and that is running. It helped me nourish my body, mind and spirit. It made me feel more alive and endorphins released made me happier.

Finally, I was able to discover my purpose while running marathons. It led me away from toxic and negative people and attracted me towards positivity. I know very well the purpose of my life is to create a positive impact in the world and this book is not a self-help book but my experiences of becoming a good human being through running. Running has also taught me to be generous and live a life with love, affection and compassion. Running has helped me live a meaningful life and it has also taught me about the importance of our wellbeing, and having a hobby, which is sometimes neglected. We live in a very stressful world today and finding time to refuel ourselves is crucial.

Surf Coast Century 2019

It was roughly around the 80km mark at about 10:30pm, when I started testing my limits. I will never forget this night of September 21, 2019 for the rest of my life. It was one of the most fulfilling moment and I lived it to the fullest. It was a life changing experience as I was surrounded by some of the most extraordinary people on the planet, embracing the joy and camaraderie of trail running. It was an unusual journey through nature, consisting of towering sea cliffs, remote beaches, national parks and beautiful wildflower hinterland.

Yes, most of my friends were busy in a rat race making lots and lots of money and I thought of doing something different. This night prepared me for an extreme adventure, or I should say prepared me for life. It was probably one of the most challenging experiences I have done in my 30 years of life. I got lost in a dense forest in the dark roughly around the Great Otway National Park. It was dark and the marking of the track was not clearly visible, if you miss one marking you might end up in another race, which probably would not finish in even 24 hours. How many of us can even think of doing such extreme adventures? In my friend circle, no one knew what Surf Coast Century was. After seeing my pictures and videos on the social media probably now they might just think of doing it in some point of their lives.

The track of the Surf Coast Century 100km Ultra Marathon was a very challenging course. It was a brutal test of human resilience and it made me cry and laugh. I met some of the most extraordinary people on the planet and this was the real test of human resilience. This was an extreme sport and normal people can die if they try such extreme adventures without proper training. I was training for six months for this adventure, but most importantly, some of the key decisions I took, kept me alive.

I kept my phone switched off for the first half of the race and switched it on at the 50km mark. Many people did this mistake of keeping their phone and Garmin watch switched on in the first half when there was sunlight. As a result, their battery went low and was completely drained out, even after the use of back up. I knew it that I would be needing my phone and maybe my support crew in the second half the most, as it would be very challenging after the 50km. And guess what I was right. I was completely drained out at the 80km mark and got bit nervous as I was not used to running, jogging or walking in the dark. To be honest, I couldn't even think of jogging or running after the 80km mark as when it is dark, you lose bit of confidence. A small mistake can cost you your life.

When I was lost around the 80 to 82km mark, I couldn't find any other runners or any red marking signs of Rapid Ascent, the company who organised this ultra marathon. I called my support crew, who were in the hotel and they started tracking me through the race map app. I texted them: 'I am lost, please help'. My support crew got bit nervous and thought of calling 000. But I guess I was at a certain stage where even God can't do much about it, forget about 000. When you are alone in the dark in a national park, trust me it might get tricky. I used Google map to find out my location but trust me it didn't gave me the right answer. I took another key decision to retreat back around 1.5km. Yes, finally I saw the red marking of the turn sign and I got the confidence. I also saw couple of other runners with headlights and it raised my confidence further. I texted my support crew that I am on my way to the last check point at the 86km mark. They gave me a hi-five emoji and finally I was on my way.

Trust me, when I was lost my heart was in my mouth. Even though I grew up watching Bear Grylls, it didn't make me a superhuman. I did come across some baby Kangaroos on my way, but I kept on moving. My aim was to reach the CP (check point)7 as soon as possible. I had to go under the bridge and then over the bridge when I was about to reach CP 7. I remember meeting two women just 100m away from CP7 and they asked me,

'Where are you from?', and they told me: 'you are an absolute legend doing this 100km challenge.' I thanked them and finally, I landed at the CP7, the last checkpoint and just 14kms away from the finish line.

People congratulated me as I reached the official last checkpoint, but when I told a woman at the CP7 that I got lost for a km, she advised me to be with someone and not be alone at this point of time in the race. I guess this was one of the best pieces of advice she gave to me.

I finally followed a Japanese runner named Shinji. But later on we got separated and it was Penelope (Penny) who stuck with me till the finishing line. I am so grateful to have met her, as she was a constant support to me and kept on asking me,

'Are you ok Suki'. I felt so good about it as in this cruel world who cares for strangers or anyone.

Yes, when I run marathons and ultra marathons, I meet some of the most legendary people on the planet. They love humanity, they love nature and they live life to the fullest. These runners were not only testing their limits but setting a goal for themselves which only a few can reach. It also helped me to be physically and mentally strong. It taught me some extraordinary lessons which I will never forget. And to be honest the track was not easy. But there is a saying if it was easy than everyone will do it.

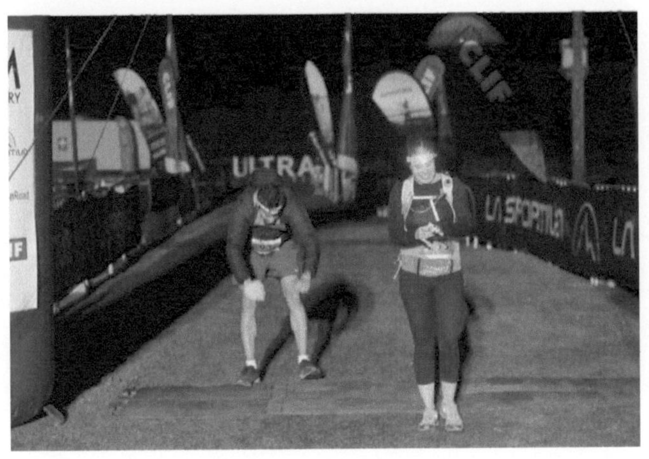

With Penny at the finish line, she supported me so much after 90km as I had almost given up

This race is no doubt a benchmark for first timers doing 100km in Victoria and is setting a whole spectrum of running ability of limitless humans. From the speedsters at the front running around eight hours, to those who have embarked on their first ultra 100km like me, this was the real test of human endurance.

The first 25kms took me along the beaches, with some nice gentle running to begin proceedings. The first leg was coastal areas with some rocky terrain and at one point there was water up to the knee. Luckily, I made a decision to take off my shoes at this point. It ended up being a good decision as once your shoes get wet, it becomes heavier and slippery.

I was comfortably able to reach the 10km mark, check point 1 in little bit more than an hour. It was really cold and windy, and I kept my Kathmandu jacket on for the entire 18 hours and 47 minutes. This was one of the key decisions I made. I saw many runners wearing and taking off their raincoat jacket or long sleeve thermal. The weather was playing the cat and mouse game it seemed. It was windy then rainy then sunny then again rainy and then again windy and at night it was extremely cold. In such kind of extreme weather conditions, you have a lot of chance of catching cold and fever. So, I thought of protecting my body in this extreme weather conditions. In fact, some spectators asked me and mocked me a little bit,

'are you not hot in the heavy Kathmandu jacket'.

I told them I am preparing my mind and body for the last 50km, as I was expecting an extremely cold night.

The jacket saved my life. After the first leg, the course headed inlands and back upon itself to the start, where runners continue into more of the inland forests for what you might deem the second loop. We finally headed to the Bells Beach at the 15 km mark and the bird rock car park at the 19km mark. The view was amazing, and I was also able to witness a

Surfing competition going on in the beach, I was running at.

Finally, I reached the checkpoint 2, 21 km mark at around 10:11am. Since the race started at 7:30am, it roughly took me 2 hours and 41 minutes to reach the 21 km mark. The first leg along the beach, I enjoyed a lot as the weather was clear and I was full of energy. This leg was basically flat from start to finish except for a few terrains over reef and rocks. I took 5 minutes break at this point and finally moved to leg 2 (21km to 49km). It was a mixture of gravel footpaths and narrow single tracks through the bushes. I remember one of the photographers was taking pictures hiding in the bush from the rain. I quickly posed for a picture and he said you have so much energy.

This leg was also not so challenging, but I was carrying a 1.5 litre sprite, which I finished in 10 minutes of the run. I was so thirsty. I refilled my bottle with water at CP3 at around 32km mark. I refilled my water bottle again at CP3A, 42km mark. I was drinking so much water at this time, as I realised staying hydrated is important for my survival.

Finally, I reached the 50km mark, which was also the finish line of the 100km solo run. And guess what I reached here again after finishing 100km at around 2:00am, the next day. When I reached the CP4, I started looking for my support crew Nancy and Hui. I was about to call them when I just saw them coming over towards me. I was so elated, and they informed me that they were here since 1:30pm, as they were expecting me to reach there a bit earlier. I took around 30 minutes break, but I didn't sit down. I had some rice, dry fruits, water and banana. I washed my face and hugged my support crew, before I departed for the next leg of the challenge. I guess the role of support crew was very crucial. It's like when the pit crew changes tyres in Formula 1 race, and these support crews were changing my gears. I didn't change my shoes or socks, but many runners were changing them as their support crew were carrying an extra pair of shoes and gears.

Since my support crew were not driving, it was difficult for them to meet me at every leg of the race. But as long as they were there, I had the confidence that someone is there for me if something happens.

I finally switched on my phone at this point and one of my support crew, Hui, started tracking me through the race map app. It was a great decision, as I knew very well how long the battery of my phone will last and I would be needing it the most in difficult times after 80km. I remember meeting one of the runners a day before in Anglesea, and he told my support crew to kick me hard at the 80km mark so that I don't give up. I just loved it when he said that. I guess sometimes the patient needs an awful tasting medicine so that it recovers from any kind of illness.

That awful tasting medicine was the last 80km to 100km. The leg 3 of the race 49km to 77km was extremely challenging as it was mostly incline. I was still jogging, running and walking at this point as I still had the confidence that I can do it. I was in a remote section of the coastal dense bushland and it was going on and on. I was just hoping to get out of this bushland so that I can see the sky.

I reached the CP6 (Moggs Creek departure), 77km mark by around 8pm. I rested here for around 30 minutes in a chair and had some amazing soup. The soup was so nice I had more. I also had some bread and cheese and water. I knew that I wasn't getting any food after this leg as this was the last big stop.

I kicked off by 8:30pm and messaged my support crew that I was expecting to cross the finish line by 1 am due to the depth of course and the darkness. I was also worried about them, as they had to move to a new hotel and had no transport. But they gave me assurance that all is well from their side, I should just focus on my race. As I moved from the 77km mark to 80km, I got a rough idea that the real exam starts now. It was the real test of human resilience.

It reminded me of the documentaries of the French Foreign Legion I used to watch. I grew up watching British Adventurer Bear Grylls, and it reminded me of how he takes crucial decisions in such extreme adventures.

The last leg consisted of an elevation of 426m. It was a hilly start but flat finish. I reached CP7 86km mark, Airleys Inlet, around 11pm. From here on there was no point of jogging or running. It was only walking along the trails. I decided to just walk for two hours in the company of Penny and we passed through the Light House and reached the Urquhart Bluff at the 94km mark.

We kept on walking at the beach and then back to trail and then beach again and finally to the point road knight beach and Anglesea main beach. Finally, we started jogging again till the finish line which was just 200m away. We roughly reached around 2 am but trust me it was 18 hours and 47 minutes of torture. Most of my friends can't drive this much without a break, we ran, jogged and crawled. We proved, is there anything which is impossible? Is there any human which is limited? We all have the capability to change the world and make an impact. I remember giving an interview at the finish line and I said,

'This is the best day of my life. I will never forget September 21, 2019. You give me a million dollars, but can you give me this finish line feeling?' I further added that most of us are going through some kind of stress and anxiety and I guess this is the best medicine. When I told some of my friends or even strangers, that I am running 100km, they told me,

'you need to see a doctor mate.'

Yes, normal people don't really run so much. But I told them you also need to see a doctor mate for not running 100km. Just imagine if all of us start running, there would not be much stress, anxiety and other mental illness. What is terrorism? It is nothing but mental illness. No one is born a terrorist but it's the circumstances which makes one. Extreme poverty, inequality results in many kinds of mental illness and trust me running, exercise, meditation helps.

I finally finished this challenge with an epic feeling and went to bed that night with great satisfaction. One of the photographers, Jayden, volunteered to drop me at my hotel and I was so grateful I met him, and we had some amazing conversation on the way. He told me just by taking pictures whole day of runners, he was so inspired that he decided to run a marathon or even an ultra marathon.

Finally, my support crew opened the door and I gave them a hug and a hi-five. Yes, it was an impossible task, but I did it. Hui helped me open my jacket and gave me some dinner which they had bought for me. It was an amazing Thai green chicken curry and rice. I loved it along with a roti.

Nancy and Hui informed me how worried they were about my location when I called them at around 81 km mark. Yes, it was a challenging assignment and I celebrated by taking a hot shower and going to bed. I still couldn't believe what I just did when I was in the shower. I remember sticking a pamphlet of Surf Coast Century in my room and I use to meditate for five minutes every day for six months watching it and visualise the finish line feeling.

My friends and family couldn't believe it but trust me no human is limited, and nothing is impossible. Everyone is a born runner, it's just that you haven't tried it yet. I met some limitless humans in my running journey, which I will never forget.

I was also grateful to have met another friend of mine, Terri McCarthy, who was there to cheer for me as she was also doing 100km relay with a team of four runners, each running roughly 25km. I am also thankful to some extraordinary spectators who were jumping from checkpoint to check-point to support myself and other runners. It was just so beautiful to see everyone supporting one another irrespective of their background, colour, race, or culture. Yes, sport unites people and we need more sports and more runners in this world.

People always ask me why do you run so much, in fact 90% of my friends don't really care whether I run 100km or 1000km, but I run for the 10% of friends, who support, me cheer for me, motivate me and tell me,

'We need more people like you'.

I am just chasing my dreams by running. My friends are also chasing their dreams, but for them success is money, power, job status, citizenship status, a big house and a sports car. But I am not chasing that. I am chasing permanent happiness and that is following my passion for running, my love for media, helping others, connecting to nature and building human connections.

Most of my friends are chasing temporary happiness and those material pleasures are not going to last forever. Your job status might not last forever, but your passion might last forever till your last breath. Steve Jobs was successful because he loved what he did. Yes, having a job is important, having money is important, as poverty is not a great experience, having a roof over your head is important, having a car is important, having a beautiful partner is important, but I am saying living life is also important. When I am running, I am living my life to the fullest. I can feel each and every cell of my body. I am in my element.

For as long as I can remember, I've been insatiably curious about human potential. I want to know the true potential of a human being and what makes people genuinely happy. Why do some people struggle while others find a way to prosper, often despite the most challenging circumstances? I know people in some of the most difficult parts of the world, who have no money, no roof, no electricity but they just have hope. And hope is a very powerful word in the English Dictionary. Trust me I just had hope that I will be able to finish this race as I know very well, many people in this world cannot do it. I was just trying to have a strong will power and determination. I was bit nervous and bit confident but what kept me going was I had hope and willingness to succeed. Everyone wants to be extraordinary, but they are doing ordinary things. How can we achieve limitless things if we are not even trying hard?

I remember interviewing the co-owner, director and event manager of Rapid Ascent,

Sam Maffett and he said to me, the Surf Coast Century is the number one thing to keep you engaged and the track has lots of variety. 'Each leg consists of 25km and is very different from other legs of the course. Leg three is the most challenging route as it is the hilliest. The tracks till the check point 6 are runnable and walkable. From Checkpoint 6, runners might feel some soreness but from there it is just getting home as runners will get satisfaction that difficult part is done,' Sam said. Sam further added: 'one will pass the Light House later on and there is no doubt that there is so much variety on the course that it sucks you on. There are 7 check points, so you don't have to carry lot of water or food. Support crew can help you change your shirt and shoes at various checkpoints.'

One important advice Sam gave to runners are that checkpoints are like magnets, but you have to get going. Even if you are walking it will eventually help you reach the finish line.

'There is progressive cut off for each leg, but there is no ultimate cut off here at the finish line. The last person might finish by 2am,' he said.

And guess what, I finished it at by 2am as I was definitely one among the last 25 people to finish this challenge.

Sam personally is a very adventurous person and he set a goal for himself on his 40th birthday and did the UTMB in France. It was 168km with 10,000m of climb. He finished it in 29 and a half hours. He came 88th out of 2000 and it was a fantastic day, the day he will always cherish.

Talking to Sam was so motivational for me as I was myself doing this 100km challenge. He gave some very crucial advice and I absolutely loved it.

Later on I spoke to Lucy Bartholomew, Australian ultra running legend, who finished the Surf Coast Century 100km solo for the first time, when she was just 16 years old. Lucy also organised a post-race yoga session and invigorating swim to kick start the recovery of runners. It was such a pleasure to meet her as this time Lucy was doing 100km relay along with her family of four, each person running roughly 25km.

Lucy told me that people who are willing to take this 100km challenge are really brave and it is something which is in all of us. 'People think 100k and it is a big number and they won't drive that far but I am super stoked to say that people are going to get a go,' she said.

I asked Lucy how her finish line feeling was after running 100km at age 16 and she replied, 'it was a lot of controversy when I ran at aged 16 as the age limit was 18 years. I was told that I have to run with my dad and do this special thing to start the race. The race ambassador pulled out because they didn't want to support the youth running. The finish line was an amazing feeling with my dad and I can't wait to do that again.'

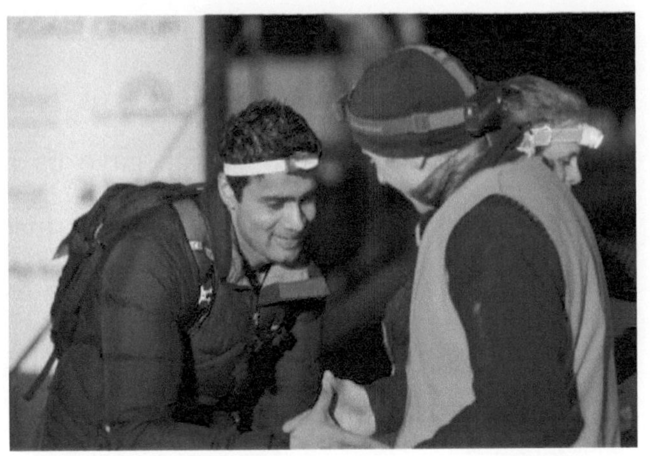

Sam congratulating me at the finish line of Surf Coast Century

Lucy finally wished me good luck before we were kicked off from the stage as the elite athlete Q&A was about to begin. All the three elite athlete and Ash Watson, winner of Surf Coast Century, 2018, 2019 and Lucy Bartholomew and Hayley Teale gave us some significant advice, describing the track and what they eat at the race morning. It was one of the most fascinating Q&A, I attended.

The traditional owners of the land played indigenous music and the Mayor of Surf Coast Shire Council; Rose Hodge gave us a warm welcome. I remember she said just arriving at the start line is very courageous, as millions of people won't even think of doing such extreme adventure.

'To reach the start line of this event is a great achievement and to reach the finish line is even greater,' Miss Hodge said.

The same weekend, the council was also celebrating the 100-year anniversary of the Great Ocean Road construction.

'We welcome both competitors and supporters to the surf coast century through our event grants program,' she added.

Most importantly, Lucy mentioned at the Q&A that there were 40% female in the event, so we need to be super proud of that fact.

'You have won the race by even just getting to the start line, by entering this event, having the balls to try something like this as most people in the world would not even dare to try,' Lucy said.

The most important advice she gave was that the first leg is full of sand and coast so don't try too hard but just enjoy it.

'Eat often, smile and just say thank you and be grateful. It doesn't make you a better person if you win and the results of this race doesn't define you. Make it great!' she added. I absolutely loved what she said.

Hearing such inspirational words of wisdom, I had to finish this race. Yes, I did finish it after nearly 18 hours and 47 minutes of torture. But trust me I will never forget this day in my life. September 21, 2019 will always remain special as I was living this day to the fullest. Endorphins released made me a happy person. I remember giving an interview at the finish line and I said,

'I feel amazing. It's the best day of my life. I will never forget September 21, 2019 in my life. It was a very challenging event and trust me the track was not easy. I have done 21 marathons, and this was marathon number 22 but one of the most challenging things I did in my life. I did 70km in the Himalayas and 60km at the great ocean road, but this was an extreme level.'

'I think the guy who finished in 8 hours is god, he is not normal trust me as no one can finish this in 8 hours,' I added thinking of this nightmare route, which was full of surf coast, national parks, hilly terrain and almost never-ending track.

I also said that just finishing this is an achievement as millions of people won't even think of doing this. 'I had made up my mind whether it takes 12 hours or 24, I will do it. I am so grateful I met Penny at the last leg, and she inspired me to kept going and she was a real support to me when I needed the most.' I guess we all need some kind of support in our lives at some point.

When asked about people doing lots of marathons is it worth it, I said,

'Absolutely, I am trying to inspire people as we need to have a running culture. Trust me all of us are going through lot of stress and anxiety and for me it is the best medicine.'

The next day was recovery day and we went to get a Chinese massage at Geelong after having some amazing lunch. My legs were sore, and the massager said in mandarin to my friend, 'no pain no gain'. I was yelling in pain as she was rubbing my feet, but she told me to calm down. After 30 minutes of massage, I was feeling a lot better and was able to walk for a while. Later on, as I got into Melbourne, I went for another round of massage as I was still limping.

Finally, after three nights of proper sleep, I felt good and recovered completely from any kind of injury or soreness. I am looking forward to the next adventure in May 2020 at Ultra Trail Australia, 100km challenge. I wish to specially thank my support crew who were constantly there to support me.

To be honest, my family do not call this an achievement. For them success is defined by my job status, how much money I have in my bank account and whether I am married or not. It's a typical Indian mindset and I never even told them that I am doing this extreme adventure, as I always love following my passion and dreams. For me such kind of challenges, helps me prepare for life. Yes, life is full of obstacles and challenges and I am just preparing myself for life when I am running such distances. It was a great sense of fulfillment for me and trust me the biggest lesson I learnt was not to give up.

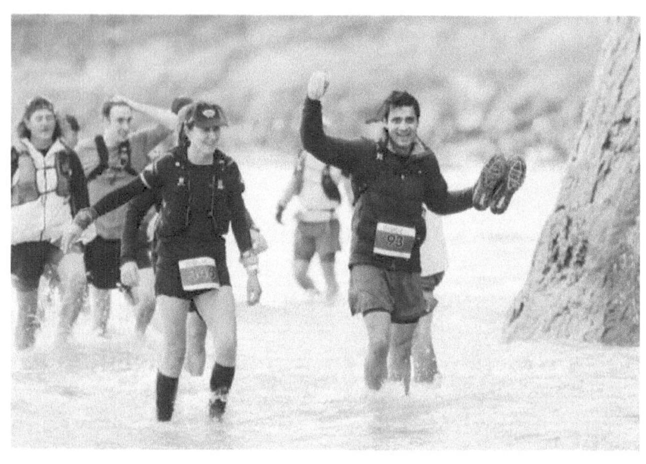

One of the key decisions I took at Leg 1 was taking off my shoes since I didn't have an extra pair

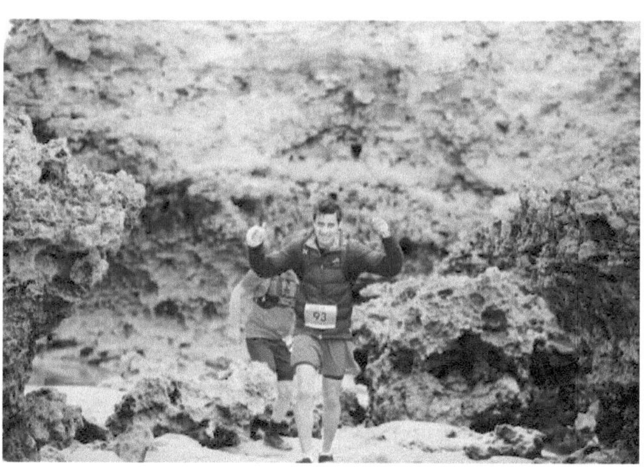

Running taught me to take key life decisions (starting leg 1 of the Surf Coast Century)

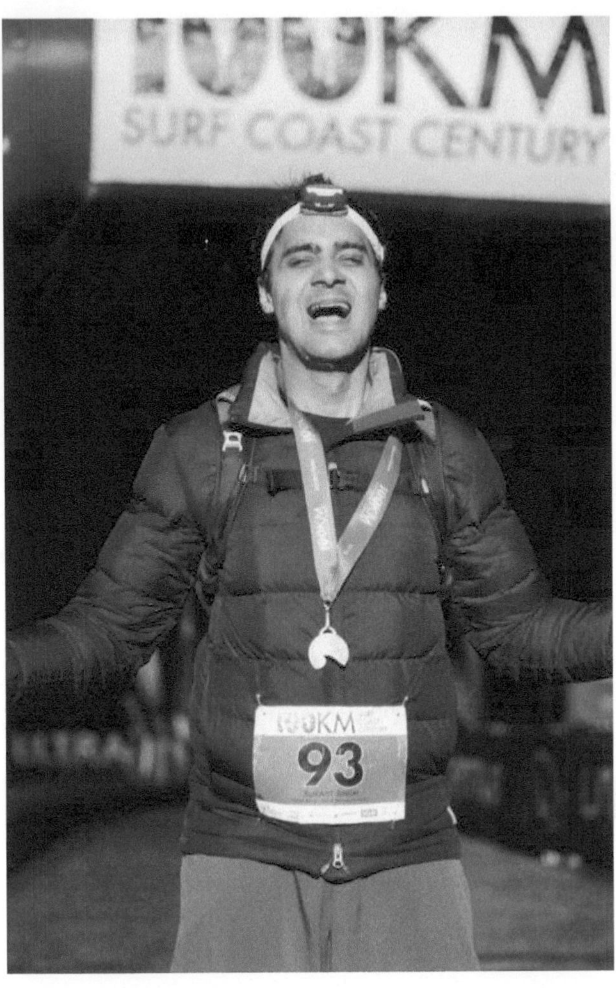

This was the feeling after running for 18 hours and 47 minutes. Can million dollars which most of my friends are chasing can give me this kind of feeling?

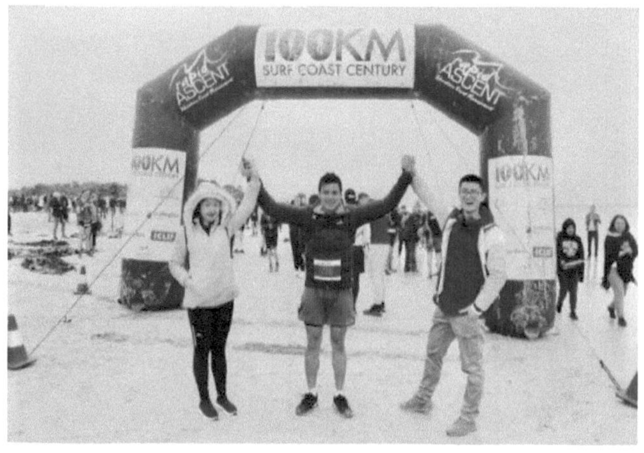

I would have not been alive today, if I didn't have these two incredible support crews: Nancy and Hui. They were tracking me through the race map app and provided me with wonderful dinner after finishing the Surf Coast Century.

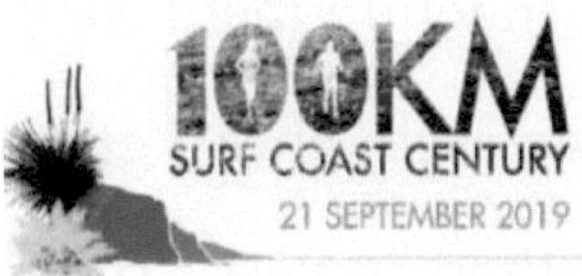

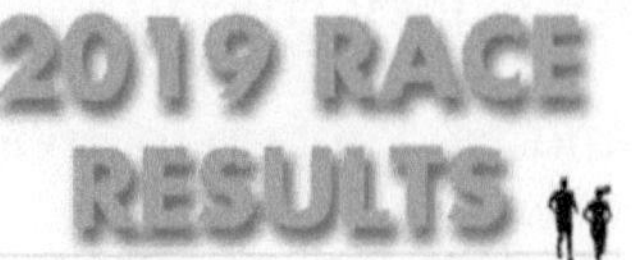

Sukant SINGH

93

Surfcoast Century

Gender : **Male**

Category : **20-39**

Status : **Finished**

★ Add To Favourites

Finish Time 18:46:01

OVERALL CATEGORY GENDER

339/35104/10234/241

Finishers' certificate of Surf Coast Century

I had given up at the 80km mark, but I kept walking the last 20km, as I knew even though you are walking eventually you will finish it. Secondly, finding a support person in the last leg is very crucial. I was grateful I met Penny, and we kept on motivating each other. I guess the last leg of any marathon is very crucial and we all need some kind of motivation and support. I generally motivate other runners and they motivate me back. It is just a norm, I follow in life, which is to help others and motivate people who have given up. It actually makes your life better and your journey easier.

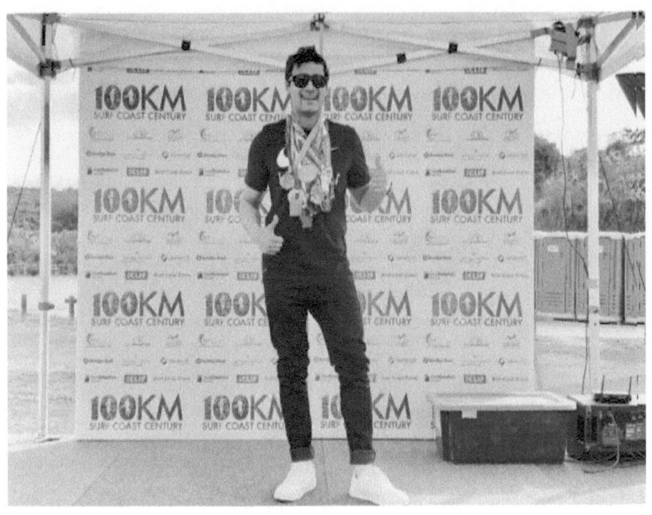

My support crew took this picture of me on September 20, 2019 with 21 medals around my neck, a day before the Surf Coast Century.

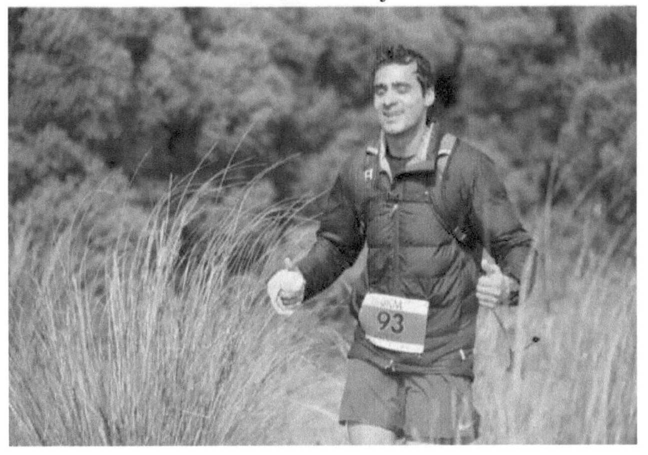

I am meditating when I am running

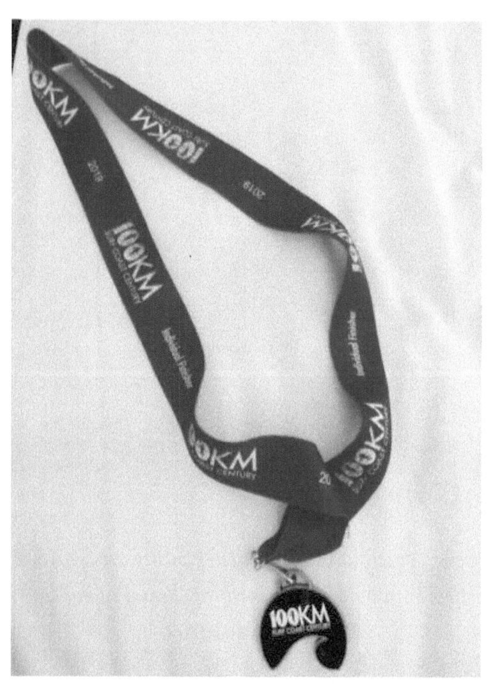

Medal number 22 and probably the one I will never forget.

Blackmores Sydney Marathon Festival, 2019 was a warmup for Surf Coast Century

It was my dream to run at Blackmores Sydney Running Festival, 2019 and I finished the 42.195km Marathon in around 4 hours and 55 minutes. About 10 minutes of improvement from last year. This was just a week before the

Surf Coast Century. I was not so happy with my timing but when I met some of the most incredible people on the planet and I interviewed some of them, I was just so grateful to be there. I came across some extraordinary people, who came from across the world for this event. Over 40,000 people crossed over the spectacular Sydney Harbour Bridge and the course records were smashed – what a day and what a feeling at the finish line. I was able to interview some amazing runners and some of the happiest people in the world.

There were over 1200 volunteers and the event was so well organised. This could not have happened without all of their support and dedication. I have learnt some incredible lessons in my life through marathons which no institution or family taught me. My school, university, parents, family, friends, work mates, even strangers taught me to build my CV; but running marathons taught me how to build life.

The suicide rates in Australia every day is really high. I am just trying to build lives and having a running culture by helping people overcome their stress and anxiety. Yes, the suicide rates are extraordinary in Australia and unfortunately never gets reported in the media (Yet, Australians are living in one of the wealthiest countries, not in difficult parts of the world like Syria, where innocent children die of chemical weapons). The death rate is predominantly high among youth males (some of them under the influence of drugs) and indigenous people who have faced brutal atrocities in the past. People from LGBTQI community, black Africans, disabled often face discrimination and it's hard for them to even get cleaning job in this country.

There are many reasons that people commit suicide. The pressure to succeed is very high and people are going through lot of stress due to their career, relationships and health issues. I am just trying to create a running revolution so that I am able to save lives. According to WHO (World Health Organization), every 40 seconds, someone in some part of the world dies by suicide, the second leading cause of death among young people aged 15 to 29 years (2019). I am just trying to save people's lives by raising awareness and empowering people suffering from mental illness by running.

I met some extraordinary people from around the planet at the Sydney Marathon, 2019, who were all running for a cause and raising awareness of issues around us to make this planet a better place.

My family, university, schools taught me to be in a rat race to make lots of money, to get a job status, to buy a big house, buy big car, get beautiful partner and according to them that was being successful. But I was chasing something else. I was chasing the finish line feeling of a marathon. Yes, I have completed almost 21 marathons by now and September 21, 2019 was my 22nd one and probably the toughest one so far and the one I will never forget. Most of my friends are chasing temporary happiness and I am chasing permanent one and that is making human connections, running marathons, helping others and saving the planet.

Just imagine if the whole world start thinking like that, the world will be a much better place. We need positive, courageous people in the world today.

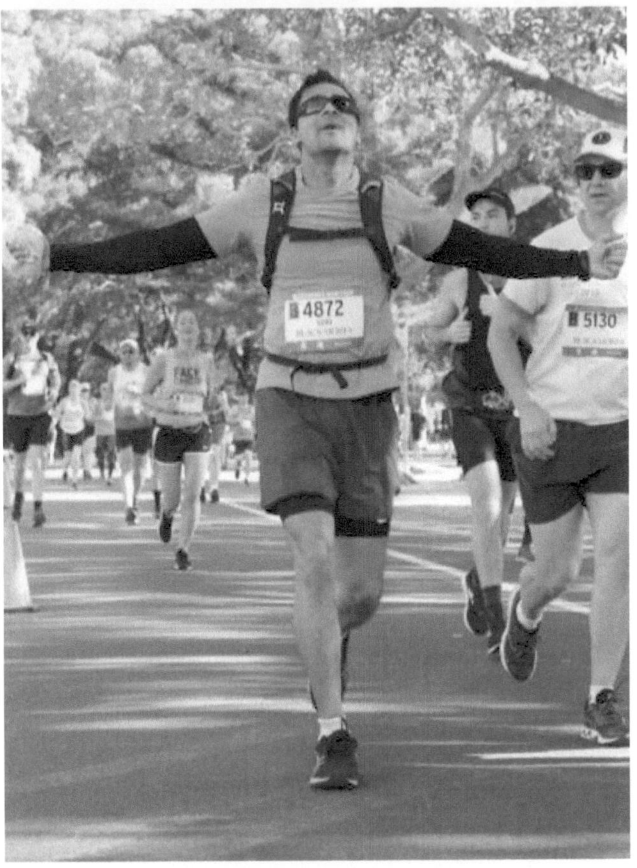

I ran Sydney Marathon in 2018 and 2019 and met some incredible people on the planet.

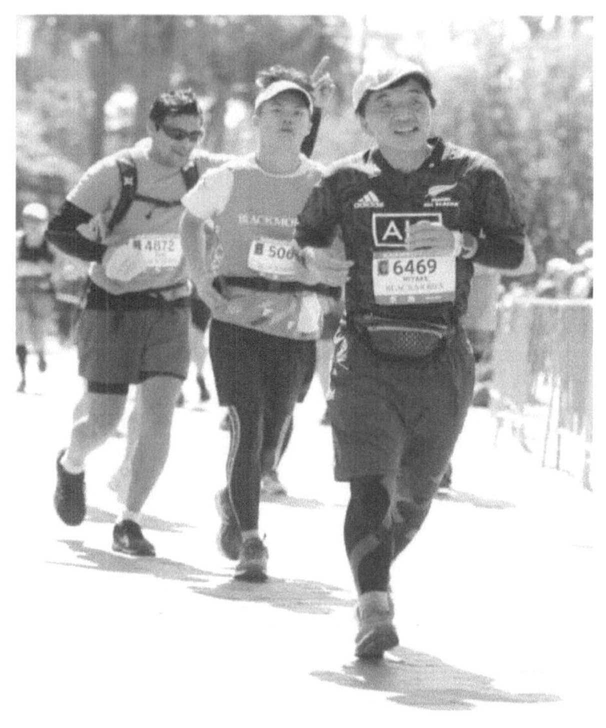

Met a great runner from Japan, who worked in the Japanese Navy and supported me in the last few kms away from the finish line.

Sydney Marathon, I had planned was just a warmup for the Surf Coast Century. I landed from Melbourne on September 14 around 2pm in Sydney. I directly went to the town hall to collect my bib and met some extraordinary runners from across the globe.

I met Dennis Boneva and her friends who flew from USA for a holiday in Australia and a marathon was one adventure they were trying. I also came across Natalia, who was celebrating her 24th birthday by running 42km. I waved to her and wished her Happy Birthday when I came across her in the marathon. I also met Ben Swee, a running coach from Singapore, who was there to test his limits at the Sydney Marathon. Ben was also with his family for a holiday. One of the most interesting guys I met was Cesar who was running the marathon with a bucket on his head, raising awareness of water crisis in some of the difficult parts of the world. Cesar have been running across the world raising a huge amount of money to change lives and make an impact. I was really inspired to hear his story. Yes, these are the limitless humans I met in Sydney.

Hearing every other runner's story, I was aspiring to finish the race in under four hours, but the weather was a bit warm, so I did struggle a bit. But compared to trail running, trust me running on roads is so easy. Like last year, the race kicked off around 7:05am at Milsons point. Passing on the pacific highway, we passed on the Sydney Harbour Bridge, then to the Royal Botanic Garden, passing Hyde Park, Flinders Street, Sydney Cricket Ground and taking turns and turns at the Centennial Park. Finally retreating back the same way we took a left turn from the Royal Botanic Garden and went to Pyrmont and finally one way back to the finish line at the Sydney Opera House.

I met a guy from the Japanese Navy and an American woman named Kathy in the last leg of the marathon. We kept on meeting again and again and motivated each other to finish the race. As usual there was a completely positive atmosphere and I unlocked my creative potential by running such a marathon. I am just trying to become the best version of myself by running such a distance. There is a saying every child is an artist but the problem is being artists when we grow up. How are we losing our creativity when we grow up?

I truly believe the education system needs a major change as they taught me to be in a rat race and get into the box of responsibilities. The school taught me to judge a person by their grades, and failure is bad. We are not defined by our grades and ranking. We all have some creative potential and schools and universities needs to be more fun, entertaining and sporty for the creative development of an individual.

I can proudly say today that running marathons taught me to build a fulfilling life. Yes, if I can inspire one individual who has given up on life, then it's worth living this life. We all are limitless humans and have superhuman abilities, it's just that we are struggling to realise it

Finishing a Marathon is a state of Mind that Anything is Possible

Finishing a marathon has been the greatest fulfillment of my life. It helps me realise who I am what I am capable of. We all are facing something today and that is called 'stress'. We are rushed by other people's timelines, as we compare ourselves to others on the social media. Someone got married, someone got better job, bigger house and better car. But I am saying why not just keep running not from our problems but for a better world.

Running releases endorphins which leads us to positive vibes and helps us overcome any kind of stress and anxiety. I believe we can never be happy if we keep comparing ourselves with others. I am friends with people who can't run even 200m and need a car or a vehicle to go to a nearby market or a gym. I am also friends with people who run some of the greatest ultra marathons in the world, which I could only dream of doing.

There are seven and a half billion people on this planet, and I am pretty sure all of us are unique in some way and have something special to offer to this beautiful world we live in. So, comparing ourselves with others is not relevant. We all have different paths, but our ultimate destination is the same. If we compare ourselves with others, we are just attracting disappointment and failure.

Some of my friends can play a musical instrument and I can't even hold it properly. Some of my friends can't paint but I am grateful I can sketch and paint to an extent. It is another hobby which helps me fight any kind of mental illness. Some of my friends love eating and I love cooking for them. It gives me a great sense of satisfaction and pleasure when I invite some of my friends for dinner and cook for them. Some people love to eat, some love to cook, some love to run, some love to walk and that is great.

My message to the people around the world is that we don't have to run marathons to be successful in life, but we definitely need to start running marathons in order to cope up with the challenges of the modern world we live in today. The purpose of our lives should be to become the best version of ourselves. To do what we love and what we are born to do. Running has always helped me realise that I am the happiest person in the world when I run an ultra marathon.

We all are facing challenges in our lives today, whether it is career, relationship or health. Someone graduated at 23 but waited 7 years to get a dream job, some had no education but was a millionaire at 18, someone got married at 20 but divorced 5 years later, someone got married at 32 and found everlasting love. So why are we in a rat race? Why not just keep running for various causes around the world for a better planet?

We all are on limited time and there is no place for anxiety, stress, or depression in our lives. We have to be grateful for all the things God has given us and be happy with that. There are no limits to material pleasure and happiness. When I run I feel like I am running for others or a better world. And that is why we are the happiest people in the world when we help others. I always believe in this

Chinese proverb in my life: " ***If you want to be happy for an hour, take a nap; if you want to be happy for a day, go fishing; if you want to be happy for a month get married; if you want to be happy for a year inherit a fortune but if you want to be happy for a lifetime, help others.*** " This proverb had a very deep impact on my life. Trust me if we buy a house or a car or any material things, we can maximum be happy for a week, a month and let's say a year. But after a year we desire for more as we humans always want more, and we will forget about the goods and wealth we inherited a year back.

So the purpose of our lives should be to help others, which gives us permanent happiness. Whether you are a doctor or a dog, the purpose of our lives is to help others. If a doctor saves lives, he/she is the happiest person in the world. If a guide dog helps a blind man find its path, it is the happiest living creature.

We humans are programmed for generosity. It is one of the best feelings to help others. It helps us grow more than we really know. When we help with an open heart, we begin to feel more empathy, and able to understand other people's lives. We need to put ourselves in their shoes and really know what they need before we help. When I try to help others, I think about how I can make the biggest impact on their lives in the shortest amount of time. I also end up building lasting relationships with couple of my friends who were always there to support me and help me in my tough times. I love this quote from Hollywood actor Will Smith, who once said: *'If you are not making someone else's life better, then you are wasting your time. Your life will become better by making other lives better.'* I absolutely love this quote as we live in a selfish world today where there is an immense amount of greed to make lots and lots of money. We forget to think about people who are in desperate need.

So, running has taught me an important lesson and that is to help others. I have completed around 22 marathons including four ultra marathons and have been running for various causes and charities around India and Australia. Every marathon has helped me live a meaningful life. In May, 2019 I ran a 60km ultra marathon at the Great Ocean Road in Victoria, Australia. This was one of the best things I did to overcome difficult times in my life.

It is said that the secret to happiness is not money but your relationships. If we have a strong relationship with our family, friends, partners or work mates then we become happy people. Running also helps me build strong relationships with strangers and of course my friends and family. I just feel like I am running away from this bad world of negativity and attracting positiveness, health and happiness.

We all our having difficult times in our lives today. I am grateful I am healthy enough to be able to run 100km, many of my friends could only think of driving that much. I believe the only way to become a marathon runner is to run a marathon.

When it comes to running an Ultra Marathon, three people comes to my mind. America's David Goggins, termed as the ‘toughest man alive’, Australia’s Mina Guli, who recently ran 60 marathons in 60 days around the world to raise awareness on water crisis, and India’s Arun Bhardwaj, who has completed bad waters in California, deemed by National Geographic as the toughest race on the planet and won the 567 KM George Archer 6 day race in South Africa.

I consider these elite runners as legends, who inspire the world to take up new challenges in life and test their limits. I personally love running, as it boosts my confidence level and I get to learn various life lessons through marathons. In May 2019, I tested my limits by running 60km an ultra marathon in Australia’s most stunning track at the Great Ocean Road along with thousands of other runners.

Our life is like a marathon, full of ups and downs that takes our breath away and the track of this magnificent race was also full of ups and downs. The race kicked off at 8am from Lorne, a small town in Victoria and ended at the Apollo Bay, another beautiful town of southwestern Victoria. I had made up a strategy of not stopping till the first 30 KM for any drinks or water in order to be able to finish it on time.

The last Ultra Marathon I had done was 70km in the Himalayas in around 12 hours in 2016. Although the elevation of this track was not so high, but the challenge was to finish it in half the time I took in 2016. As we passed the Cumberland River Lookout and Mount Defiance Lookout, I was elated enough to be able to reach the 10KM mark in an hour. We arrived the 20 KM mark at around Separation

Creek and Wye River and I had my first protein shake, which I was carrying on my small bag pack. Later on we moved to the Kennett River and Cape Patton Lookout, passing through Wongarra and finally, finishing at the Apollo Bay.

I am so grateful to have met a runner named Michael Zajer who motivated me to finish the 60 km challenge. The distance roughly from the start to finish was around 44km but since I was doing the 60KM Ultra Marathon, I had to take another turn at 47km mark to an extremely elevated route of around 10km. Discerning the elevation, a thought came into my mind that, I might not be able to finish the race in the cut-off time of 6 hours and 30 minutes.

When I was just thinking of giving up, I met Michael, an Ultra Marathon runner, who motivated me to go further my limits since we still had two hours remaining to the cut-off. I was so grateful to him, as I would have not been able to finish this race, without his support. He was like a messenger to me from God, who just came to inform me that 'I can do it'.

Similarly, we never realise our full potential unless somebody tells us. Why do some people need to hire a personal trainer in the gym, why people need life coaches, students need teachers and why do even successful people need mentors? The internet has all the information in the world we need but we still need someone to motivate us, push to our limits, so that we can come out of the filter bubble and achieve our goals.

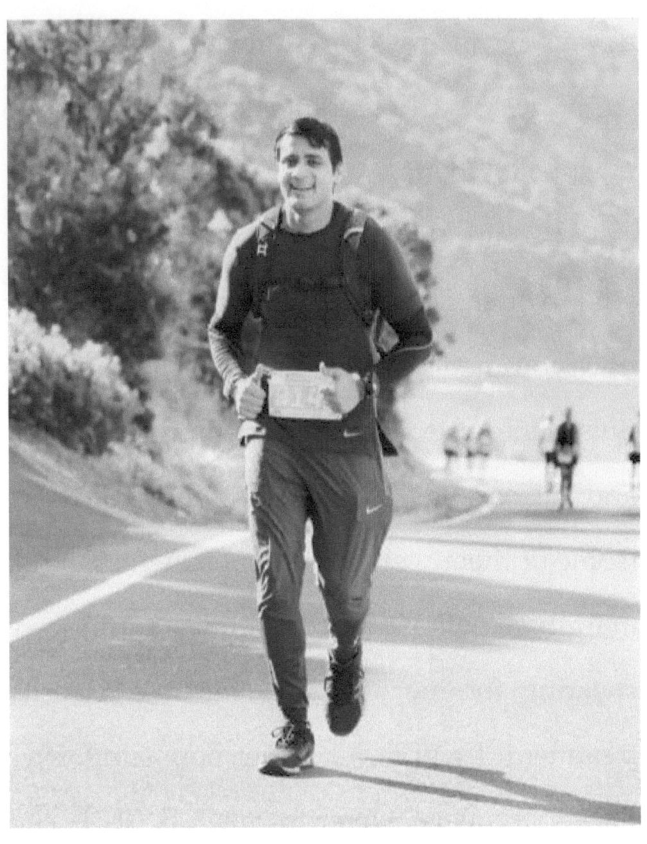

Finished Great Ocean Road Ultra Marathon, 2019 (60km) in 6 hours and 30 minutes

I met so many other runners, who not only motivated me but also shared their running stories and that kept me going. To be honest, I have completed several marathons till now, but the Great Ocean Road Marathon will always be in my heart forever. The kind of support I got from strangers; a simple hi-five meant a lot to me.

It is said that people will always forget what you gave them, but will never forget how you made them feel. When I crossed the finish line in exactly 6 hours and 30 minutes and 50 seconds, people at the Apollo Bay (some of them were also runners, who ran full marathon, half marathon and even ultra) were cheering for me and gave me the celebrity treatment. I will never forget how supportive these strangers were to me, as if I had achieved a lot in my life. To be honest, I haven't achieved much in my life right now but running 60km definitely raised my confidence and finishing this epic race made me realise that anything is possible. I dedicated this memorable run to my late mom whom I was seeking energy from when I was in so much pain. At times, I was even chanting the Tibetan Mantra *'Om Mani Padme Hum'* for energy. I strongly believe that these powers will give me instant energy.

Like any other race, the last 5km to 7km is always difficult, but to get over it I tricked myself into thinking that I was running 70km and not 60km. It eventually helped me. I am so grateful for all the support I got from other group of runners at the finish line, who helped me sit in a chair and offered me some bananas and water.

The biggest lesson I learnt was that it embraces us for a new challenge. 'If it was easy everyone will do it', what makes you special is how you prepared your mind to achieve your goal. Another lesson is that self-discipline will get you farther than motivation will ever will. Waking up early and going for a run in an extreme cold weather is not easy and not everyone can do it. But if we prepare our mind to get up early and go for a run the night before then we probably don't need an alarm clock. And the most important lesson, running long distances is 10% training plans and 90% showing up. Trust me, for most of the marathons I did was without proper training. People didn't believe me when I said that but once I showed up on the day and meditate a night before the race, I am able to do it. The real battle is fought above the shoulder, in our heads. Running along with thousands of people automatically helps me keep going. For me running marathons is a meditation and is one of the most enjoyable adventure.

I generally motivate a stranger during the race and that person eventually motivates me back with a simple hi five, which gives me an instant energy. This is a very common strategy I use while running a marathon. But if we are competing in a race or planning to win or get a decent position, then we definitely need to train hard. I often run on the treadmill in the gym, sometimes even 20km in order to avoid the rainy weather outside. But for running long distances, I would often recommend training outdoor and on a hilly terrain.

Running long distance also makes us resilient and prepares us to cope with the challenges of the modern world. We live in a world today which is full of challenges and mental toughness is the need of the hour.

I have never seen a successful person without a difficult past. If we just Google it or search on YouTube, we would find probably hundreds of stories of people who become something from nothing. We all have faced rejections in our lives and I always believe that if we get what we want its good, but if we don't even better. Well it is a positive way of seeing life, but the most important lesson I have learnt while running is how to be optimistic when the world is against you and you have been rejected by the world. Whether it's your family, friends, partner, work mates and even strangers, if you have been ever rejected by them, there is nothing to worry about. It is said that people can be alone are always stronger than people who always need company. Why not we start loving ourselves so much without caring about the world.

Why do people commit suicide? Whether it's the indigenous people in Australia or the poor farmers in India, the suicide rate is very high because people from these communities feel that they have lost everything in life, and they have no hope for their future. But I wish I could just tell them to go for a long-distance run and see how they feel afterwards.

Running not only empower us but helps us fight anxiety and depression. Lots of lives could be saved in this world if we encouraged our family, friends and mates to start running. I am not telling you to just start with 26 miles or 42 km marathon, but one can even start with a 10km run. Trust me it's very addictive and once people motivate you and praise you, you will only go farther and farther. We have to be just positive and persistent as it is a long journey.

I always believe that comfort is the thief of progress and if we are living in comfort than we can never progress. Our life is full of challenges, in fact as long as we are alive there will be challenges. The most important thing is how we cope with these challenges. I believe what Steve Jobs said: 'Sometimes life will hit you in the head with a brick, don't lose faith'. We all have been hit in the head sometimes in life and it is up to us how we prepare our mind and body to recover from that injury.

I started running at the age of 18 to cope with the modern challenges of the day to day life and have never stopped since. I believe running has not only helped me become a better human being but has also helped me adapt to extreme conditions, stay motivated and become a better decision maker. A research conducted by the Forbes found that one in four CEOs suffer from depression. It is very true to say that extreme successes have many strings attached and it can pull a person down completely. The point I am trying to make here is that mental health is a big issue around the world at the moment and it is costing a lot to the economy.

So how do we cope with the modern-day

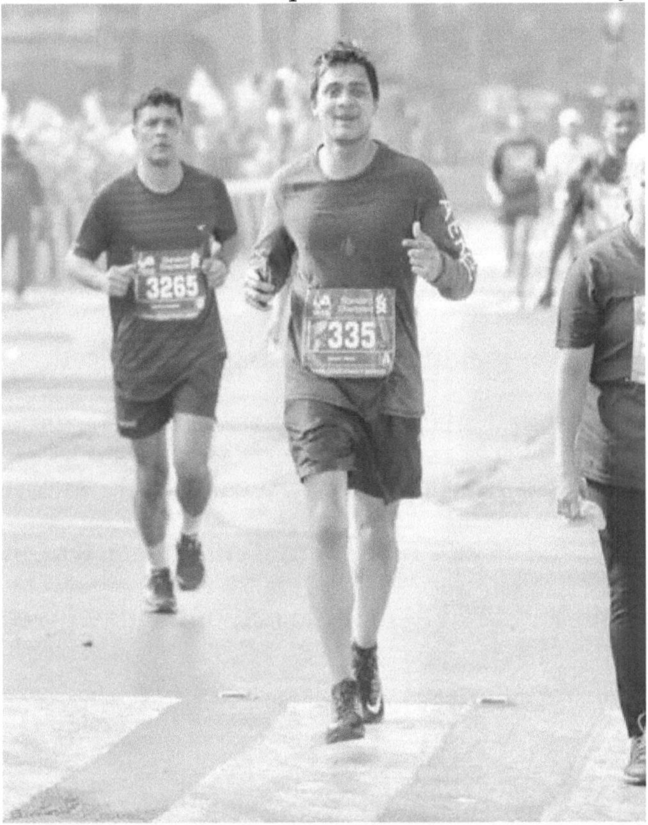

stress and challenges, and become better leaders and decision makers?

Mumbai Marathon, 2016

I personally advocate running as a great solution to this problem. Having myself successfully completed a few marathons in the last few years, I have learned to prepare my mind to carry out physical obstacles. The science behind running is that interval running trains our muscles to use oxygen more efficiently. As a result, as soon as we read something after some exercise or running, we grasp information more efficiently and effectively. Our decision-making power also gets enhanced.

My first marathon was standard chartered Mumbai Marathon few years back and I finished it in 4 hours and 8 minutes. I was in pain and tired, but at the end of the day I was glad that I did it. Later on, I started training for ultra marathons and I successfully completed the 50 km Bangalore Ultra, moving on to the Shimla Ultra marathon of 70km in June 2016. I ran my latest marathons in Melbourne, Sydney, Gold coast and it's my dream to run New York and Boston one day and test my limits.

Every time I run, I feel like I am high on something. Running is meditation to me, and I am proud to be a runner. I like running because exhausting myself is the most relaxing moment for me. Running is not only therapeutic but also an awful tasting medicine which helps me recover from anxiety.

People may think I am a lunatic for running so much but I believe that it's imperative to chase one's passions and dreams. Every marathon I run, I also test my endurance and limits of human resilience. I always test myself to see how far I can go. Meditation can help us to perceive things differently and so our potential can grow.

Running for me is not only a sport but also a lifestyle. It helps me stay focused and listen to my inner voice. I wish to run for various causes around the world and inspire myself and other people on the way. In January 2019, I heard about an Australian Ultra marathon runner Mina Guli, who ran 60 marathons in 60 days across the world. Her mission was to raise awareness on water crisis around the world. I could only wish to be fit and be able to run like her. I feel if we all take one issue close to our heart and start running and raising money for various causes, the world will no doubt be a better place to live in.

The challenge is how to convince people to run. I can only be a role model for people and help them in their running journey. When I see professional athletes who run long distances, I always wonder if they are normal human or super-human. We all have some super-human abilities and it is just a matter of realisation. The only person inside my brain is me and I do not let other people's opinions get into my brain. Nobody in the world knows better than me what I really want in life. When I told my friends, family or even strangers that I will be running 60 km or 100km, they got goosebumps and didn't believe me. They thought I was fooling around and its unachievable.

Nelson Mandela said, 'everything seems unachievable unless somebody has done it'. If tomorrow, I tell my neighbour's or work mates that I am going to climb Mount Everest, they will probably laugh at me. But I believe there is no need to tell anyone what our goals and plans are because no one in this world knows better than me what I truly want in life. If I am suffering from anxiety or depression no one else is responsible for it but myself. I was able to hold on to people's opinion on me in my head for so long, as I was unable to break out of those thought patterns until I started running. People will always love you and hate you, whether you are a celebrity or a common man, there will always be people who hate you and love you. If we start thinking of all the people who hate us, then we can't live.

When we fail, we often start giving excuses and blaming others. For example, if I was not able to finish my marathon in my desired time, I would often blame the weather for being too cold or too hot, I might blame the track for being hilly or curvy, I might blame other runners for being not supportive, I blame my injury or my diet or I just say I ate wrong food or a drink which made me feel sick. I can bring out 100's of excuses for being not able to finish the marathon in my desired time. But admitting my failure is the best thing I can do to focus on my future runs.

I recently did an Improv workshop in Melbourne in which we were taught to says, 'I have failed' and everyone will clap over it. So, admitting failure is the best thing we can do to overcome failure. Nobody likes failing or rejection but accepting our failure is the best way to move forward towards success. So, there is nothing wrong in admitting our failures. We only post pictures of our good moments on social media to attract attention. But celebrating our failure helps us move forward. In other words, rejection is just a redirection. People have been able to change the world because of rejections and failure. If Steve jobs was not fired from his own company, he would probably have not changed the world and created something which we all use it today. I love this quote from movie Steve Jobs. The Apple Co-founder Steve Wozniak after listening to jobs contribution asked Steve Jobs,

'You are not an engineer, neither a designer nor an artist, what is that you actually do?'

He responded by saying, 'Musicians play their instruments and I play the orchestra.' It means that we all have the ability to play the orchestra in our lives. God has given us some unique talents and it is up to us how we use it.

We should never let other people's opinion shape our future. I have the ability to redesign my brain according to my abilities. We all have different abilities and we all are unique in some way possible. Some can run 10km, some can run 100 km, and some can even run 1000 km, and that is completely fine. We should never compare ourselves to others on social media. We all have different timelines but one thing we all share is death. At the end of our lives we should be able to achieve our goals. For some people their ultimate goal is to make a fortune, for some the ultimate goal is to make an impact in the lives of others. I believe in making an impact in the lives of others by doing what I love and running long distances. Running also helps me become a good human being. I love running even more when strangers at the finish line support me and cheer for me. I feel like I am making this world a better place by running. While running alone helps but if we are running with some of our mates, it's even better.

We all need some kind of encouragements in our lives. Imagine people living alone their whole lives, it would be very lonely. You can have all the money in the world but no one to have dinner with. We all are happy not just when we are surrounded with money but with good and positive people. It is very essential to surround ourselves with positive people who would help us achieve our goals. Similarly, if we are running with someone whom we share some connection, it always enhances our performance. We always need someone to share our stories with. Asking for help or sharing our problems is not a sign of failure but a show of strength and confidence. We all have learnt some lessons from difficult times. If we haven't faced difficult times, then we would most likely never learn to work hard or embrace ourselves to the challenges of the modern world.

I have been through bad times when I had less than $10 in my bank accounts, I felt there was a need to change to improve my financial situation. The difficulties that I have faced in my life, especially after the death of my mother at the age of 12, has made me even stronger. The most negative period of my lives became transformative and the greatest blessing. I realised I need to stand up and do something impactful. The twelve-year-old boy in me who was weak and bullied at school didn't last for long, but the 30-year-old in me was a mentally strong person. And this was possible only because of running. If I never played any sport or got into marathons, I would have never learnt some significant life lessons.

Running is like meditation and a therapeutic medicine which helps me keep anxiety at bay. I always wanted to do something which impacts the world. I wish to be a voice for change and a role model for people. But since I came to Australia from India, I was failing again and again. And I feel that is pretty normal. Whenever anyone asks me, why do you run so much, is it your job? Why not be a normal human being and just get a normal job, get married, buy a house, have kids and then wait for your turn to die. I always knew that I will never follow the crowd. I wanted the crowd to follow me, to become a leader and share my knowledge and wisdom which I have learned by running various marathons.

The Great Ocean Road marathon taught me various lessons like when someone tells you, you can't, it means you can. Whenever I told anyone that I am running 60km they didn't believe me. They questioned my ability to run, they asked me some weird questions, have you even trained for it? The track is hilly? Are you sure you can do it? These doubts reminded me of Arnold Schwarzenegger who said: '**ignore the naysers**' and yes, I did ignore them. Why I am letting other people's opinion shape my future? If I am stuck just thinking of the criticism of other people, then I can't move forward. I realised that I can do it, so I meditated the night before the race, and it helped me complete the marathon in a record time of 6 hours and 30 minutes and 50 seconds. So, the second lesson I learnt was to never follow the crowd.

When I came to Australia in 2016 as an overseas student, every student was in a rat race and they studied mostly IT, accounting or nursing. They thought it's a short cut to getting permanent residency, and it was easy to get a job since those subjects were on the skilled list as per the Australian Immigration Department.

I chose a different field; in fact, I chose a long path to success. I studied International Relations, which is not in the skilled list, but I enjoyed every part of it specially the media units. The biggest lesson of my course was that global problems needs global solutions. I was just thinking to myself, if I am able to take one issue which I am really passionate about and start raising awareness with the help of my runs, the world would be better off with minus one problem. Whether it is corruption, climate change, terrorism, poverty, inequality, slavery, trafficking, water or food crisis, I feel we all have an obligation to do something about these issues. Well I can't change the world in a day with my runs, but I can definitely change myself for a better world. And that is what running has taught me.

Another important lesson I learned while running long distances is I need to be able to share this wisdom or knowledge with the people who are suffering from anxiety, and make them aware that fitness promotes health and enhances our quality of life, and is an important factor in overcoming or managing these illnesses. It makes us more confident human beings. It also helps us take crucial decisions in our lives. We should also stop over thinking. It takes a strong mind to stop us from over thinking and focus our attention towards positiveness. Of course, fitness is not the only factor to improve our mental health, but it has helped me a lot.

Practicing yoga and meditation is one way to help you focus on your goals and help you to become a better person. I am meditating while I am running. We all have bad days at work, at school but the more we ruminate about that, the more we develop neural pathways of negative thinking that can lead to some form of anxiety. I develop positive thinking by doing two things in my life – when I am running, I generally chant a Tibetan Mantra called "Om Mani Padme Hum". It means that in dependence on the practice of a meaningful path, we all have the ability to transform our body and mind which is impure into a pure mind and body of Lord Buddha. While I am not a very religious person, I do get attracted towards Buddhism in my life which talks about self-less sacrifice, generosity and other good things to make our lives more meaningful. These Buddhist prayers are generally carved into rocks, prayer flags and prayer wheels in India and is a popular form of teaching Buddhism.

Every time I chant these mantras, I get some kind of instant energy. I feel empowered, I would say chanting once every 100m of my race gives me the equivalent energy to a red bull or any energy drink. I generally practice this form of prayer and meditation while I am running and almost in the last leg of my marathon. Running the last

10km of any marathon or ultra marathon is a difficult task. It is the time, when we have lost all our motivation, ran out of energy drinks and there are only a few people left to cheer for you. At this difficult moment, when I am in so much of pain, I just feel like praying and thus the mantras works. I feel like there is an outside force which is willing to help me in every way possible to reach my goal, which is the finish line of a marathon.

I try to focus on my attention on my goal with my thoughts. I always believe thoughts become things. I am determined that no matter what happens whether I die or crawl or crumble or walk or jog, I have to finish the race. If we have poor opinion of ourselves or we think that we are not good enough or shape our mind by the noise outside then, of course we cannot finish the run, whether it is a marathon, or it is our life goals. My positive self-esteem has an impact on other people's lives. When I inspire people and motivate them to finish the race, when they are in so much of pain, I am making someone else's life better. But the good vibes are reciprocated, and as a result my life becomes better. I get energy to run further when I share my energy.

Similarly, our knowledge improves by sharing our knowledge. Our happiness improves by sharing our happiness with our friends, family and even strangers. So, the biggest lesson here is to share our wealth, happiness, food, water and even motivation with people who are in desperate need.

Our running capacity also depends to a large extent on our diets and the way we think. I am not used to smoking or drinking, but I did have a bad habit and that was my addiction to soft drinks. I used to drink a coke a day on average. It was very addictive and used to take it more often, especially when I am stressed out. After reading about the harmful effects of Coca-Cola, I switched over to Sprite. Slowly, now I have become addicted to coconut water and fresh juices. I would not recommend juices from the supermarkets which has added preservatives, but instead drink fresh coconut water from raw coconuts also available in the supermarket, and drink fresh juices from the juice shops or junctions. It's a good source of energy and a way better than soft drinks.

Secondly my thoughts create a huge impact on my running abilities. Meditating for even 5 minutes a day can help us calm down. I realised I became more positive by meditating, eating healthy foods, surrounding myself around positive people, going to gym, cycling, swimming and even painting a canvas once a while. We all have a great human body and we have to fuel it with positive energy to function well. My thoughts can either destroy me or change my life for good. Why do I just focus my attention on the 18 people who do not like me? Why not focus on 100 people who inspire me and like me and consider me a good human being? We can't force everyone to like us and that is cool. I am sure many people after reading my book may not like it and criticise it, and I am pretty much sure many people out there will love it and motivate me to keep running and writing. So it is very important to surround myself with those that are good for our mental health.

As we get older, we will realise that wish we would have started running earlier. The mind always fails in running before our body gives up, so it is essential to convince our mind to keep going. There is a beautiful quote: 'If people put as much effort on running instead of hating others, there would be lot more marathoners and the world would be a better, loving place.' We have to accept that there is no place for hatred in our lives. We all can change our lives by attracting positive vibes by running long distances.

People always see success like an iceberg. We all share our success, finish line photos, medals on the social media but we never focus on the hard work our athletes undergo like sleepless nights, good diet, self-discipline, 5 am runs, expenses, time managements, determination, tears, and disappointment. So, we all need to undergo a training process which enhances our performance.

One of the greatest benefits of running for me was self-awareness. Running marathons made me realise who I am, and it gave me power to listen to my inner voice. Our inner voice is very unique, and it should help us stay true to our values and goals. Steve Jobs has said: 'You are already naked. somehow you already know what you truly want.' If we are able to listen to our inner voice, it somehow has solutions to all the problems we are facing today. Whether it's our god, our parents, elders, past and present, before listening to them, we need to listen to our own inner voice. I do often ask my inner self to provide me with strength, wisdom, new ideas, opportunities, spiritual and mental growth. My heart should say to me that yes, I am doing the right thing.

We should all have the courage to follow our heart. Because if we are doing anything with our passion success is inevitable. Whether you are black or white, tall or short, or LGBTQI, most of us have the ability to run and improve our lives. Self-awareness also helps me realise what I am passionate about. I am passionate about media and keep myself updated to the news and happenings around the world. Today, I am still relatively young and lack bit of clear vision, but I know that I want to make a career in media and television. I have a deep passion for it. I am myself when I run, paint and cook. These hobbies help me listen to my inner voice. The better we know ourselves, the better it would help us realise our full potential.

Running for me is not just a sport but a passion and a way to live life. When we are alive our lifeline is curvy with ups and downs just like the track of our marathons. When we are dead our lifeline is straight. So, running marathons helps me realise that I am still alive and there is a reason why I am alive. We all have come up against a brick wall in our lives. You know those times, when you are struggling to find enough physical energy to move forward in running or in life? Mentally we just have to refuse to give up and finish the race. Running hurts, me but it's one of the best feeling you can have at the finish line. How does one feel after climbing Mount Everest? Those feeling can't be described in words. After having sleepless nights, struggling days without proper food and water, and breathing less oxygen, when you reach the highest peak in the world, it's a great feeling. There are no limits to what we can achieve in our lives. Similarly, we have to overcome the fear and do something different. Can we become a confident human being by staring into the face of fear? Can I overcome pain which will trouble me in every phase of my life? Can fear give me in writing that I will fail? Can we make our liabilities our assets? The day we are able to make our liabilities our assets, fear will go away. We all have to understand what is defeat and that demon inside our head which tells us we are not good enough.

Whenever, I say my big dreams to people around, they laugh at me. Which I feel is pretty normal but there are also people around me who believe in my dreams. When I run long distances, I am totally out of my comfort zone. The pain in my body orders me to give up at certain stages of a run but what keeps me going is my self-awareness and visualisation. I always try to conquer the run in my head and visualise the finish line. I could only see people congratulating me and I feel like it's my day. While defeating failure is not an easy task, running helps me always keep chasing for more. When I first ran 10k, I always wanted to run half marathon. When I finished half marathon, I decided to run a full marathon 42.195 km. When I finished the full marathon, I started thinking of Ultra Marathons. I ran 50km, 60km and 70km and finally 100km. Now I am planning to run 200 miles Ultra Marathon in Western Australia called Delirious West in some point of my life. So, there is always something which helps me keep chasing my goal. I'm always coming up with new goals. If I am able to run 200 Miles then probably, I will think of doing 7 marathons in 7 days in 7 states challenge, then Iron Man triathlon or cross-country run. So, there is always something to chase and I will never reach my goal easily in life. We have to stay hungry and keep chasing our dreams like long distance running.

Training in Cairns, Queensland for a big challenge

We have to keep chasing success but having a strong mind is also important. When someone ask me why do you run so much, are you

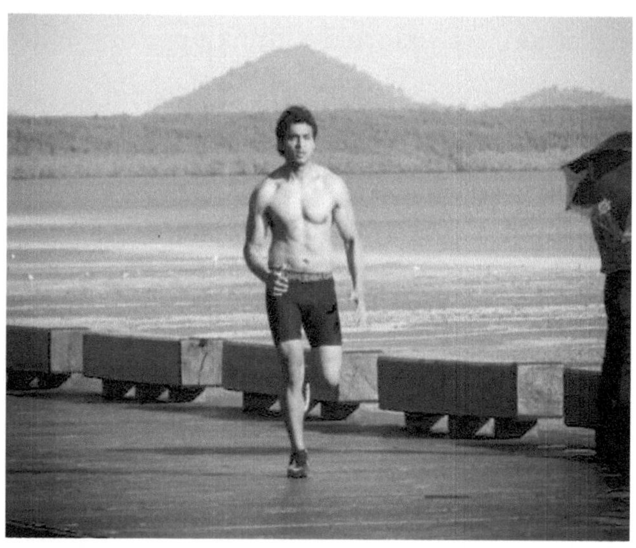

crazy? I say to them I am preparing myself for life. As motivational speaker Jay Shetty says: 'As long as we are alive, life will crush you, squeeze you, crumple you but we should never lose our spark, our values within us. A dollar will always have the same value no matter if we make it dirty or crush it or squeeze it, similarly we will always keep or values within us even though life is not treating us well.'

I know very well how it feels to lose a loved one. I lost my mother at a very early age and the day is not far when I might lose another member of my family. We all have to die one day but we all want to live a meaningful life. We live in a world today when we might not just lose a loved one but get fired from a job, or suffer from some serious health issues like cancer. Some disease can happen to anyone and if we are healthy, we have to be grateful for it. Life will always hit us with a brick, the question is are we prepared to catch that brick. I keep my body and mind strong so when I wake up with bad news, I am mentally strong to overcome any challenges of life. Life is a gift and we should all embrace it and not take it for granted.

We all get to live once so why not take care of our body and mind. When I run I meditate. For some people running or meditation is a waste of time. For me it is a way to live life.

Creating space and time for running has provided me with lots of answers. Running helps me get clarity and vision. I do get positive energy which I bring into my everyday life. I always plan to go for a long run once a week. But sometimes, I am not able to find time for outdoor runs, so I instead prefer treadmills in the gym. I do try to eat and drink healthy, although I do have lot of cheat days. I end up eating butter chicken and chicken biryani, one of my favourite Indian dishes. It has lot of fat, but it tastes delicious. I do try to make it up after eating something unhealthy by going on a solo 40km or 60km run. But running does not generally helps me lose weight. So for physical fitness is: 70% diet and 10% work out, 10% sleep and 10% mindfulness and lifestyle.

There is a saying that goes: '*Let food be thy medicine and medicine be thy food*'. The simple meaning is, if we are consuming fast food and processed food, we can't expect to be free from any diseases. The medical professionals will always advise lot of drugs to recover from mental and physical illness, but I am just saying why not just keep eating healthy food consisting of lots of green vegetables and fruits and keep running. We should definitely avoid certain fruits and vegetables we are allergic to. Science has proved that one of the major reasons for anxiety and depression is the wrong kinds of food, like the fast food we are eating today. I do treat health as a matter of life and death. It's easy to get bulging biceps but the important thing is what are we actually consuming. I do believe that we need to live a meaningful life by eating right and exercising on a regular basis. There is no shortcut to success and similarly there is no shortcut to living a healthy life and running long distances. We have to change our mindset to live a healthy life.

I come from a middle-class family and I always think in a simple way. I want to eat something cheap and simple. I try to be consistent with my running, diet and exercise. If you are not disciplined and not living a healthy lifestyle, you will not get anywhere. If we are eating healthy and running, our performance at work also improves. I often meet people in the gym with six pack and ripped with muscles. But they can't even run 5km. It surprises me and they are shocked when I tell them my running story. I am saying if world leaders have time to meditate, practice yoga and go for a run, so do we. I know world leaders around the world who get up at 4 am or 5 am and do their workouts or yoga and read newspapers in various languages and finish their workout before breakfast.

Just like I am always hungry for getting my dream job, I am also hungry to help others and do something for humanity. Running teaches me that I have big responsibility on my shoulders, and I have the ability to save lot of lives of people who are suffering from anxiety. I often find people when I hit the gym with strong muscles. But are they healthy or fit? Are they mentally strong? Are they ready for a challenge in their lives? Are they consuming supplements to boost their muscle? Are they consuming processed food and junk foods which has harmful chemicals, leading to mental health issues?

We have to accept that we need to be healthy and not just fit. Having a six pack does not necessarily makes us healthy but running 100km does helps us become healthy. I believe if we have some potential or talent to inspire others, why not use it to change lives. My goal is to improve my timings of runs and qualify for Boston and New York Marathon some day, and finish it under 3 hours or 2 hours and 30 minutes. We all should stay hungry and always aim to improve our timings in marathons.

Running at the Great Ocean Road festival, described as Australia's most stunning race event, also taught me some meaningful lessons. I was running along with 8200 other runners who completed various categories of race. I smiled and was grateful to be able to enjoy one of the most magnificent view. I realised that my peace is more important than thoughts driving me crazy, trying to understand why something happened the way it did. I forgot all my problems and just focused on my run with other great runners. I realised that nobody can side-track me when I am trying to reach my goal. I felt like I was sitting in the driver's seat and learning how to climb over unexpected humps that came along my way. I realised that I have to stay resilient in this journey for 6 and half hours and every mistake I make is an opportunity to make better informed decisions. It should not let me make same mistakes again and again. I was preparing my mind to take next step in my life and was thinking of every obstacle as an opportunity. I felt like the whole universe wanted me to finish this race. I was always looking for an opportunity to have a conversation with a runner and it eventually helped me cover some miles with ease. I was thriving and finding success through feeling energetic and excited, when I was challenged.

I had made up my mind to run with my full potential. I was not running because I had to post pictures of mine on social media. I was running because it made me feel good and so

I realised that trying to appease everyone, fearing change, living in the past and overthinking will not lead me anywhere. The world already has enough critics so why not be an encourager? I started encouraging every other runner around me and I wanted them to finish their race as much as I wanted that for myself. Another important lesson was to let our legs do the running, our mind do the pacing and our heart do the pushing. If we are doing anything from our heart, whether it is our job or any sport or hobby, we can do great work or create great things. I always run from my heart and mind more than from my legs.

Another lesson was to give back to the community. Hundreds of people supported me in my race, I am so grateful for that. I always love helping people. It gives me an epic satisfaction. Sometimes, I might not be in a position to help others, but I do have couple of friends who are always there for me when I am in trouble. My father didn't support me in my runs at first, but later on he started encouraging me to run more. I guess, I come from a poor village in India, where people even don't know what a marathon is. Well running marathon is not my career but a hobby, which helps me live a meaningful life. I never blame my parents as they always want the best for me. I believe if they have left me with their problems, those problems are mine now and I have to find a suitable solution. My father always used to put pressure on me to succeed. He being a cardiologist, his relatives and colleagues expected me to be also a doctor. But I always believe that doctors and engineers are not the only successful people in the world. We should have the courage to follow our heart and do what we are born to do. I could be a world class runner, painter, journalist and a writer. We all are creative in some way and we just need to mind our paths and keep running towards our goals. I do get a lot of confidence when I run and I realise that our mind is a muscle and we need to train it every day so that we can become smart. There is no doubt that our thoughts create things, and in order to stay positive, I practice meditation. If my thoughts are bringing positive vibes, it will reflect in my actions as well. I try to surround myself with positive people and I always follow gratitude. I am always grateful for all the opportunities I got to run. I am grateful, I studied in one of the best schools, got an opportunity to study abroad and my mother always taught me whether you achieve anything in life or not, become a good human being. Do something for the planet. I wish to spread love and kindness through my runs. There is no place for hatred or jealousy in our lives. It is damaging for our mental health. I am grateful, I was raised up being a good role model of how people should treat one another. It's my dream to run 100 marathons in my lifetime and set these good examples and send messages to the world. Crossing the finish line has been the most fulfilling moment for me. No matter how many times I have done it, it makes me feel incredibly great. Running has made me realise that, there is nothing wrong in being yourself. We all have some defects, nobody is perfect and the world will love you for who you are. We don't have to change ourselves too much to fit to the expectations of the society. We all just need to become the master of our skills and keep doing what we love.

I also get some spiritual learning while I am running. One of the lessons I learned is that as we go, we have the ability to give back more. If you see an ocean and someone is drowning, you need to help them. But if you are not a trained swimmer and you made a decision to save the life yourself, probably you will get drowned as well. So, when I am not able to help, I will seek for a lifeguard to save life of the person who is drowning. Similarly, in my life, if I cannot save someone else life then I would not spend time with the people who will bring me down. I have to find someone who can save that particular person.

And I have realised that I cannot change the life or improve the life of every dead soul but if I am able to inspire even one, it's worth living. We all have the ability to change our lives, but we just need to understand the importance of our dream and what is our priority to reach greatness. Is making millions of dollars our priority, or is it serving humanity? For some, greatness would be running an ultra marathon; for some greatness would be climbing mountains; for some greatness would be the work they do as a nurse, doctor, lawyer or journalist. But are we able to move mountains every day in our work?

I was one student who never had a clear vision and I studied International Relations. You could be diplomat studying that or also an author, journalist and entrepreneur. I have seen people even becoming an actor after studying International Relations. So, we have to see the possibility of greatness, before we dream it. Having a clear vision is very important and I got the vision by running various marathons.

Secondly, I always visualise and think, 'What if I was the greatest actor in the world or an athlete, how would I react to that situation?' So, it all starts with thinking like the world's greatest mind, training like the world's greatest minds and helping others and becoming a philanthropist.

Running taught me to never give up.

Running has taught me various life lessons. Every marathon, half marathon, ultra marathon I ran taught me an important lesson. To be honest there are no rules of running. You can run in the coldest place and even in the rain and at 40 degrees Celsius. There are no limits to how many miles we can run. But we all have different capabilities and there is nothing wrong in that. As long as we are running and filling our life with such adventures, we will be happy, as running releases endorphins and it could be a game changer.

My 11 Rules for Running

In running don't compare yourself to other runners.

Often in marathons, I have met some elite runners who can finish a 42km run in under 3 hours, which is a pretty good timing for a marathon. The winner of the Sydney Marathon, which I ran in 2018, finished it in under 2 hours and 15 minutes, while I took nearly 5 hours to finish the race. There were also other runners who took even longer than me. So, running is a sport not to be compared with other runners and participants. Similarly, in life I follow my own timelines and comparing myself with my social media friends would not lead me anywhere. When I discovered running as a hobby and a break from the stressful world we live in, I initially found it tough and then got into the swing of it over a period of time. In the ten years since I ran my first marathon, I have completely become obsessed with it, and it is a form of meditation for me. I have always considered marathon, not as a competition, but an adventure. So, there is no point of comparison.

Help other runners. It's my favourite thing to do.

I believe we are programmed for generosity and that helping a mate when they are tired and about to give up, will eventually enhance our performance. A simple word of motivation or a pat on the back could help someone finish the race. This would give us pleasure, and we are actually helping ourselves by helping other runners. Distance running is sometimes a lonely pursuit and there is a risk of self-doubt coming into our heads. The mind is telling us to stop when we are tired and eventually, we stop at the drink station for a break. At that time, we just need some mental energy. The energy drinks and water can give us physical energy to go for another mile, but mental energy we can only get by a simple touch or work of motivation. When I was running Gold Coast Marathon in 2017, someone told me: 'You got this mate, keep going'. It completely changed me from negative emotions to positive emotions. I was grateful I was able to finish the race with the enormous support from strangers and other runners. I always advocate to have the right mindset, whether when we are running or in our daily lives. This mindset eventually helps me keep going when I am tired or in self-doubt. Our mind is equally important as our legs. I often practice meditation in order to improve my brain muscles. Like we go to gym to build our muscles, our mind needs rest and proper sleep. If our mind gets tired in a marathon, it could be only refueled by motivation from strangers, other runners, family and friends. Similarly, when we are mentally sick, we need love, compassion, motivation from loved ones and sometimes even from strangers.

Tap here to power up.

A simple hi-five or a smile, or a creative poster with motivational quotes could give some energy to our brain and help us reach our goal. Positive mantras really work well for me. As I had mentioned before, the

Buddhist prayer, 'Om Mani Padme Hun', really gives me energy and I do often chant, when I am running. When I am running long distances, I do worry at the start about how I might be feeling when I am 10 km away from the finish line. The last leg of any ultra marathon is not easy, and we can only stop worrying by focusing on the present moment and banishing negative thoughts from our heads. I acknowledge the negative thoughts and try to replace them with positive mantras.

You don't have to go too fast, as long as you are going.

When I am running ultra marathons, I do not worry about the time so much, as long as I am able to finish the race. Although we may need to care about the time, if there is a cut-off and we are expected to finish the race within a desired time. What I am trying to say is we do not need to start too fast, so that we get tired quickly. As long as we are even going slowly after 30km, it's fine to be able to finish the race. If we are competing, then we might need to focus on our timings.

I always say this prayer when I am in pain, whether it's during a run or in life: 'I will remain focused on my goals. Even if I face a moment of difficulty or a setback, I will not give up. I know consistency is the key to success. I know that I can do it. It's natural for things to not go to plan. But the challenge will not block me. If I commit to the process, it is only a matter of time. I am grateful for all the opportunities I got in life.' This prayer brings me towards positive vibes, and I get the feeling that I am not tired and can keep going. I also prefer shorter goals as a pathway to reach bigger goals. I first started running 10km, then half marathon, later full marathons and now Ultra Marathons. I always try to schedule my runs in advance. I treat it like a meeting, which mentally prepares me to turn up. I prefer long runs on the weekend, and some work out at the gym in the weekdays. Such slow training prepares me for bigger challenges. I do love cycling and swimming as well, and it eventually helps me prepare for triathlons and Iron Man. It is my dream to compete for an Iron Man sometime in future, but I am not a great swimmer, so I need to prepare hard for it. One step at a time.

Be positive, be patient and be persistent. It's a long journey.

Running marathon is a long journey. On average, I take 4 hours to finish a marathon, and if I am running ultra marathons it might take from 6 hours to 18 hours sometimes. So, it's definitely a long journey and staying positive and motivated is the key throughout the journey. Lots of negative thinking comes into my mind when I am close to the finish line but being persistent and continually working towards my goal is very significant. Basically, we have to work hard in silence and let our achievements be the noise at the finish line. I am the happiest person in the world when I reach the finish line.

People have often given me negative vibes, but I trust myself. Every single person, including my family members do not believe it, but for me running 50km is now like a walk in the park. But I am now training for some serious challenges, which would help me become mentally strong and of course, a good human being. I always believe that because we only get to live once, pursuing our passion is very important. Running is passion and a hobby for me and even if I am able to run long distances once a week, I would be able to refuel myself for the rest of the week. Just like we put fuel in the car to be able to function properly for a week, similarly, I go out to run in nature once a week to refuel my body. It helps me become more patient and compassionate. In August 2019, I ran 50km and 53km in the last two Sundays in Melbourne. I ran for nearly 7 to 8 hours near the Brighton Beach.

A few days after, I ran 60km by myself. It was very much tiring, but I could easily sense a feeling of satisfaction. I felt that I was alive and that there is a reason why I am alive. I often run to lose my mind and find my soul. Yes, we live in a hectic world today, where we often lose our soul. We forget our capabilities and achievements, and fear of failure makes us suffer from stress and anxiety. We never share our failure on social media, but we love sharing our new job status, achievements, citizenship status, marriage or purchase of a house or a car. But we forget to share our failures and the days we are feeling low. I have rarely seen a very successful person, maybe a celebrity, actor, politician or CEO, without a difficult past.

All of us have gone through some kind of challenges in our lives and it's time for us to share it on social media, instead of sharing positive moments. I was reading an article recently and watching news on TV and I came to know that 1 in 4 people in Victoria, Australia, is suffering from stress, anxiety and depression. Suicide rates, predominantly among young males, are high. I realised that there is something seriously going wrong, where money has become so significant in our lives. We are treating money and job status or power as a symbol of success. We treat dogs better than humans. If I go to a supermarket in Australia, I will probably find a large variety of dog foods, dog party mix and their clothes, electric blanket.

We have dog police, veterinary doctors and so many other facilities for dogs. There is nothing wrong in caring about dogs and treating them nicely, but have we lost humanity and stopped caring about the person sitting next to us in the train who might be suffering from mental illness in silence. There are so many people in Australia suffering from mental illness and pressure to succeed is very high. Some suffer this disease which is invisible due to their career or relationships or health issues. But very few of us really care for others as we all are in a race to succeed. I truly believe the purpose of our lives is to save other people's lives. No matter what we do for our living, we all have the capability to do it. Sometimes a simple smile or a hug could change people's lives. Staying positive and consistent, when the whole world is falling apart, is very important.

We all have been hit in the head by a brick in our lives and the hardest paths have also the ability to make us strongest. Often, we go to gym for a month with a mission to have a body like Arnold Schwarzenegger but give up after some time. We forget how much focus, dedication and discipline is needed to achieve that dream. Everyone has a dream but very few have the courage to follow them. Running long distances have taught me that it's not about how fast we run but how long we stick with it. So, it is a long journey and remaining focused is very important. Often, we lose our focus or decide to give up on our dreams after several rejections and failure. I just remember the shark experiment, whenever I am dealing with any kind of failure or rejection. I have been rejected several times when I have applied in Universities to study or even for jobs.

We all have faced rejections but if we all can remember this shark experiment; it could have a deep impact in our lives. During an experiment, a shark was placed in a large tank by a marine biologist and small bait of fishes was released on the other side of the tank. As expected, the shark jumped on the fishes and ate them as quickly as possible. As it was easily available, it was an easy job for the shark. But as soon as fiberglass was placed in between the tank in order to divide two sections, the shark was not able to eat the new bait of fishes. The shark kept on slamming the glass and bounced back. It kept on repeating this for a while with no success, while fishes kept on swimming on the other end of the tank unharmed. This experiment was repeated several dozen times over the few weeks. And later on, the shark became less aggressive and eventually stopped trying all together.

A few weeks later the fiberglass dividing the tank was eventually removed and to everyone's surprise, the shark didn't attack the fishes. After experiencing repeated failure, the shark was trained to believe that the barrier existed between it and the bait fish, so fishes swam unharmed without being attacked. The moral of this story is we all have faced constant rejection and failure in the past and so our brain automatically gets programmed that this real barrier still exists in reaching our goals. Even though there have been barriers in the past and we have failed, we should keep working towards our goal and not stop dreaming big.

The only way to become a marathon runner is by running a marathon.

Many of my friends who struggle to run even 5km, often ask me how do you run? My simple answer is if you want to become a marathon runner, first register for 10km or half marathon near you. If you turn up that day eventually you will be able to finish it. There would be hundreds of people running along with you and it would eventually motivate you to keep going. And trust me, it's very addictive. I have been running for 10 years now and when I meet some amazing people at marathons, some extraordinary people, who tell me their running story, I feel more motivated to continue this passion. Yes, running marathon is very adventurous but it also tests our mental and physical capacity. But trust me, the feeling at the finish line with arms raising in triumph, is simply amazing.

When I ran 70km in the Himalayas and 60km at the Great Ocean Road, I didn't train properly but I realised that meditating in our mind is more important than anything else before a marathon. Then comes the diet and our sleep. I ensure I get an 8-hour sleep and light dinner before the marathon. Running your first marathon could be challenging, but once we finish the first one, trust me there would be many more after that.

Self-discipline will get you farther than motivation will.

Every morning when I get up, I get easily motivated by watching an inspirational video, but I realised that self-discipline is more important than motivation. The day I get up late, I feel lazy, while the day when I wake up early, I am full of energy. So, preparing my mind to get up early is the biggest battle I go through every day.

Suggesting to my mind not to eat junk food, even though I am surrounded with junk food, is the biggest battle. When I am running, I do give lot of pain to my mind and body and my friends and family often wonder why I am doing this. Why I am giving myself so much pain when I can have an easy life. But I am training my mind to be ready for life challenges. I do follow the teachings of the Dalai Lama and he says, when you have met tragedy in life, you can either lose hope or be hopeful, and running has prepared me to be hopeful.

My mind often tells me to eat more and run less but I try to convince my mind that if I don't run, I might die, but if I don't eat unhealthy meal portions I might survive. So self-discipline comes by convincing our mind to do things we love. We all make new year resolutions to eat healthy, go to gym, read books or earn more, but how many of us have been successful in keeping those promises. To be honest, I have never been, but I do prepare my mind to run more every year.

Also, the biggest lesson that running taught me is to be calm when the whole world is against you. When I came to Australia, I got some great opportunities to work in Coles supermarket, Monash University and even at the Australian Broadcasting Corporation. But I also ended up flipping burgers and chicken for less than the minimum wage and was often subject to abuse and racism. That time I wanted to take revenge and approached authorities for help. But to be honest, after nothing much happened, I kept thinking about the bad experiences again and again, which eventually harmed me the most.

Our thoughts become things, and I was more suffering from stress and anxiety due to these negative things in my mind. So, I asked myself, 'When people abuse me and call me a loser, am I able to maintain my cool?' People in our lives, whether at work or school, often lose control and abuse us and distract us from our vision. But if we keep thinking about that over and over again, we can't move forward. It has always happened with me but running has taken me towards positivity and I believe every challenge is an opportunity. Self-discipline has also taught me to make the right choices in life. Running a marathon boosts my mood and increases my productivity and it also helps me to make right choices in life.

If people put as much effort into running as they do into hating others, there would be a lot more marathoners.

I live in a world today where people love me and also hate me. I know very well that no matter how great a human being or successful person I will become, there would be someone who will not like me and that is fine. I can't force anyone to love me or like me and I always prefer to be myself. So, the most important thing is to be myself. My family never supported me completely in my running journey. They wanted me to have a decent job, get married and have bunch of kids, then probably buy a house and car and wait for my retirement. But that was their dream. My dream was to make an impact on this world before I die. I realised I have this skill of running and I can inspire people to run marathons and become more positive.

Running gives me great confidence and makes me realise that anything is possible. I have often come across people who think I am not following the norm by running so much. I have also come across people at university, school and at work who never liked me and tried to bully me or make me feel low. But I realised that if I am putting so much effort into hating them, I am harming myself. There is no doubt that where my attention goes, it grows. If I got fired from a job or I lost some one in my family, I cannot move forward if I am thinking about it again and again. We all have been in relationships, some are good, some are bad. But if I ever had a bad experience with a person, it takes me a while to forgive the person and move forward. The sooner I forget the incident, the better it is for my mental growth. I know very well, I have greater vision in life, and I do not want any hater, toxic people to make me lose my calm or focus.

I try to instead focus on my goals, my physical fitness, diet and health, which would help me grow and accomplish my goals. I want to put my entire focus on my running, and it would eventually help me forget all negative energy (hatred, jealousy, revenge) inside me. If I can focus on other people to start running marathons, I would not only be able to save lives of people suffering from stress and anxiety, but also there would be more marathon runners. Running has also taught me that it is not just about hating others, but our purpose is to serve, give respect to others and give back to the world. The former President of United States, John F. Kennedy once said: 'Ask not what your country can do for you, ask what you can do for the country.' I clearly resonate with this line as I believe there is no point of my education, if I am not able to make an impact, save lives and contribute to this fast-changing world.

I consider myself to be privileged enough to be able to study in a reputed university in Australia. I studied International Relations with some core units of Media and Communications. I have a great enthusiasm for Media, Film and Journalism, as I believe they have the power to shift culture and form public opinion. I wish to use my education in giving back to the under privileged world. I am very well aware some people live in very difficult parts of the world, without proper education, food, water or housing, and trust me, poverty is not a very good experience.

People suffer from various kinds of mental illness due to extreme poverty and I am grateful, my situation is a lot better than theirs.

I realised, I have everything to be grateful for. But sometimes, when my attention goes towards negative stories, I do suffer from fear and stress. Due to my background in journalism, I love watching news on TV. But sometimes, when I come across some disturbing news on Facebook or on TV, it really upsets me and makes me feel low for few days. I am pretty sure journalists come across some of the very difficult stories related to crime and drugs, and it could impact their mental health. At the same time, interviewing some of the world's most extraordinary people and famous people is also a rewarding job. But I have recently tried to consume less media content as sometimes it might consume us, and we might become more fearful and anxious. Media has the ability to form public opinion and today I still love media, but I consume its content in a limited manner.

I remember watching the Australian Story episode that focused on Mina Guli, who ran 60 marathons in 60 days. This was a really inspiring media content. Such stories should be highlighted, creating a positive impact in our lives. I love watching movies as well, which inspire me and are based on true life events. The more I consume positive content, the more I attract positive people in my life. I am a big fan of British adventurer Bear Grylls. I love watching his show Man vs Wild on the Discovery channel, which is one of the most watched show on the planet. I recently watched the episode in which he interviewed former US President Barack Obama and Prime Minister of India, Narendra Modi in nature, around wildlife and natural habitats.

Such media content keeps my adrenaline running and motivates me to run often.

Whenever I run marathons, I come across some extraordinary people who are leaders in their field. I like running in nature, as some of the runs I did in the past were in the forest. I recently did a half marathon in Victoria, Australia, called the Forrest Trail Run.

According to English dictionary, 'trail' means a beaten path through the countryside, and if the word 'running' is added to it, it becomes an adventurous sporting activity which combines running and hiking on steep gradients and unpaved surface. I wasn't much aware of trail running, until I experienced one. I was fortunate enough to experience 100% pure trail running at the Run Forrest Race, held at a village situated on the banks of the Barwon River and located roughly an hour drive from regional city of Geelong and nearly two hours' drive from Melbourne.

I am so grateful to my two new mates Katryna and Simon, who informed me about this adventure, and we decided to do the 21km (half marathon) challenge. The race kicked off at 10am which gave us plenty of time to drive from Melbourne to the starting point, where we collected our bibs. It was a cold Sunday morning and I realised that the temperature was even lower than expected, by seeing a km long queue to take a leak at the few temporary portable toilets set up for the event. While Simon and I decided to relieve ourselves in the bushes as we couldn't wait for that long, Kat (Katryna) patiently waited in the queue and finally her turn came very close to the starting time of the race. In fact, the organizers of the race delayed the start for another 10 minutes, observing the queue of people waiting to relieve themselves.

We started the trail run following the Barwon River along the famous Red Carpet to Lake Elizabeth at around 10:10am. It was one of the most magnificent experience of my life. I felt like I was inside a video game or a movie like *Jumanji,* surrounded by ferns, on a covered single track, and fast downhill corners giving us the feeling of a rollercoaster ride.

We hiked and jogged through the beautiful fern surroundings, past the majestic Lake Elizabeth and experienced several cambered turns and fast down hills with great sense of energy. The trails reminded me of the rollercoaster marathon I did in Dandenong two years ago, although it was much easier compared to it. There were three water stations along the route: one at the 5.5km mark, the next at 8km and the final one at the 16km.

I was so glad to see some amazing volunteers at these water stations, who were also there to ensure the safety of all the runners. While trail running sounds very adventurous, it could also turn out to be deadly if the weather is not that great. At around halfway mark, I saw a giant tree completely uprooted and blocking the trail, perhaps due to heavy wind or rain last night. I was grateful the weather was very pleasant while we were running, and a bit sunny, as we progressed throughout the day. We were roughly able to finish the race in under three hours. Among the three of us, Simon was the first who finished the 21km challenge in around 2 hours and 25 minutes, followed by me and Kat.

Along the way I met some amazing other runners who also ran the Great Ocean Road Marathon with me in May 2019 and joined for Surf Coast Century later in September 2019. Alan, another runner I met during this trail, informed me that he really liked my blog on running 60km ultra marathon at the Great Ocean Road. I definitely felt honoured, and this kept me motivated to keep running and keep writing. While I have completed roughly 20 marathons now, every marathon is a lesson not just to be fit and healthy, but it teaches me how to live a meaningful life. Often after every run, I do a simple mistake of eating a lot, as I generally fast before the run. It works for me, but I do not recommend this for other runners, as all of us have different food habits. This time I had decided not to eat too much but have something light just after the race.

Luckily, a soup festival coincided with the event and was located at the Forrest Football Oval.

The 'Otway Soup Festival' featured some homemade soups, pickles, homebrew beers and wines, books, art, clothes and a fresh market stall. In fact, in the name of soup, there was almost everything available for sale. We enjoyed the lentil soup and some deep golden fried potatoes in the form of spiral. It was a great recreational moment after a wonderful run.

The best thing I like about running in mother nature is that it brings people together. It crosses boundaries, culture, language and helps us feel united with positivity.

A marathon will help you discover your strengths, you never knew you had.

There is a saying, *Once in a lifetime, one will find a hobby that will change everything.* Yes, every one of us is doing some kind of a job to pay our bills. But I am asking what are you doing to realise your full potential. We all have some kind of hobby or unique talent, but are we able to find time to explore it? Some of my friends, when they have a job title or power, they feel confident; some of my friends when they have a bank balance, they feel confident; some when they go to gym and build muscles, they get confidence; some when they sleep or do yoga they get confidence; some when they eat the food of their choice or spend times with their loved ones they feel energetic and elated. I get confidence when I run ultra marathons. I am the happiest person in the world at the finish line of a marathon. It also gives me confidence that if I can run long distances like 60km or 100 km, I can do anything. Everything seems unachievable unless somebody has done it.

I believe pain makes us stronger, fear makes us braver and failure makes us better. Running marathons is an important part of my life. It can teach us how to live a purposeful life. Life is full of challenges and obstacles, and running a marathon prepares us to overcome the challenges of our lives, whether it is our career, relationships or health. I remember running often and posting on social media. It is not always that I get positive comments from my friends and family. Some supported me and some were critical of my passion. For some of my friends and family members, having a job status, money and power is more significant than running 100km. I come from a small village in

India, where there are only two professions which are considered to being successful – Doctors and Engineers or Civil Servants. I love neither of these professions so basically, I was considered a failure.

While I am not a doctor who saves lives, I am a runner who is able to save lives by inspiring people to run. I realised God has given me this unique skill and I can use it to inspire people who are suffering from stress, anxiety and depression. It helps me recover from any kind of mental illness. It is a hobby which I am very much proud of. It teaches me to face struggle but never quit. Every marathon I did, it taught me to fail. Yes, we all want to succeed in our lives. Nobody wants to be poor, trust me it is not a great thing, as it leads to mental illness. But do we have the courage to fail? It is my dream to run marathons and ultra marathons in some of the extreme places in the world. But obviously I need to be financially strong in order to being able to fulfill this dream.

People have called me a failure and have given up on me, but it is very important for me to believe in myself. Every time I run, I become more positive in life. Running is a meditation and makes me realise that through all the hard work I did, and even though I haven't been able to achieve what I want, I am not going to give up. I still have hope, as hope is the most powerful word in English dictionary. I am at the brink of something great.

The hardest run is running alone, but it also makes you strongest.

Running has taught me how to enjoy my own company instead of expecting someone else to make me happy. Yes, we live in a world today where technology has become our priority over people. There is so much noise from parents', society's, partners' and friends' expectations. We are feeling lonely sometimes because we are not able to connect the dots with the people around us. You might be very different and unique from the rest of the people around you. We don't always have to think inside the box.

The things that have helped me improve my quality of life is by doing what I love, surrounding myself with positive people. It's better to have a couple of great friends than 1000 friends on social media, who are not happy to see you succeed. Having a clear vision and focus, working hard, being creative, spreading positivity, taking risks and staying away from drama, have helped me a lot.

You might have the most expensive house in the world, but if you are eating dinner alone in that house, trust me it is not a great thing. Loneliness is equal to smoking ten cigarettes a day. It could affect our mental wellbeing. But it is also believed that people who are alone are always the strongest.

The biggest example I can think of is my dad, who never married again after the death of my mother in 2002. He has been lonely since and trust me being lonely at old age is not very great for our health. We all need a life partner who encourages us, support us and help us when in need. Trust me, I cannot run alone 100km, although I might be able to do 50km alone. We all need motivation, encouragement in our journey.

I have often met some amazing support from strangers, which makes my life much easier while running long distances. The human body is capable of achieving limitless things and our possibilities are endless. This is what running has taught me. And most importantly, I have met limitless humans in every marathon.

A strong person alone can also achieve limitless things. It's just a year ago that I was watching the training of the French Foreign Legion, one of the most brutal military assault courses on the planet. The training prepares armed men to survive in the toughest situations on the planet. It also helps them to make crucial decisions at various stages under pressure.

Some of my favourite shows are Canadian-Australian adventurer Todd

Sampson's *Body Hack* and *Redesign my Brain,* in which Todd trains with soldiers in the Amazon forest. It is so inspiring that I felt like everything is achievable even when you are alone. The ten-day test called toughen up is designed to test the resilience of soldiers in the French Foreign Legion. When I run marathons, I feel that my job is much easier than this training.

Running 42km is not a big deal compared to the training of the legion. In the training often some soldiers reach a breaking point and give up. But sometimes the hardest kind of training teaches us some great lessons. Every failure is a step closer to success. For many people, just running a marathon is a big deal. For me running 100km is a big deal but it is my dream to run a 217 km ultra marathon called Down Under 135, which is one of the toughest courses in Australia.

It takes two days of non-stop running but hopefully I will qualify for that race by being able to finish Ultra Trail Australia 100km in the blue mountains in New South Wales. These are big dreams and I prefer to stay positive and focused in my running journey. I do also care about injury, as all dreams could be shattered, if I don't take precautions and injure my legs. I run alone sometimes for many reasons, but it always comes back to self-satisfaction. And finally, running alone makes me realise that we all need to remove that voice of self-doubt inside our head.

The best way to recover from injury is to run more.

While this running rule might sound bit inappropriate, it works for me. To be honest, there are no rules to running. You just have to register and turn up on the day of marathon and have some belief in yourself. Some people take a rest after a marathon, but I prefer to hit the gym and do some recovery exercises. It eventually helps me recover. Of course, we need proper sleep and food after running long distances but running on treadmill and doing some squats in the gym also helps me recover from the pain.

Every one of us are different so people might have other ways of recovery. One thing I always observe that we have lot of life coaches, personal trainers and yoga gurus who call themselves influencers and try to create positive impact on people's lives. But my question is, 'Are you practicing what you are preaching?' I am a runner, and if I am writing a book on running, I am expected to run a few marathons.

I love to take actions and inspire people by my work and not just give speech. Many of my friends who cannot run even 10km, when they see my post of social media, they get a hope that if I can do it, so they can as well. I inspire people to come out of their comfort zone, give something a go and ignore the naysayers.

I remember injuring myself seriously at the 70 km Himalayan race, and at the 21km challenge in Mount Dandenong in Victoria. It took me few weeks to recover, I couldn't afford to visit a physiotherapist, but I went to gym regularly and rubbed my knee over the roller. It eventually helped me recover from the injury. Similarly, we might also be injured in our lives, not always physically, but mentally. A tragedy might strike in our lives and it might be difficult to recover from it. But the more we run and take care of our physical and mental wellbeing, the more we will be able to recover from tragedies. If you just focus and never give up, you will overcome every obstacle in life.

Pain is one thing, suffering is another: suffering happens in the mind. Once you detach from that, you can handle the pain. And it makes you tougher and stronger. There are so many success stories I have seen, whether it is of a celebrity, an actor, or a sportsperson. They all have suffered from hard lives and have come back strong. Through practice, hard work and more importantly through research and education, anything is possible. We need to believe in ourselves, when the whole world is against us. Experience teaches us a lot in life. Every marathon I run is an experience, and it is preparing me to accomplish something big in life. It helps me to find resilience, strength, understanding and awareness. It also helps me know that life is just like a sport, and we need to play it well.

Every time I wake up before a marathon day, I am full of curiosity, enthusiasm and excitement. I am never unhappy. I have experienced anxiety, stress and depression in my life, and we all go through ups and downs in our lives, but the most important thing is to keep moving forward. The ups and downs in our lives are like the track of a marathon. We have to just keep moving along the track with a clear vision or destination in mind. Every adversity comes with a blessing, we just have to find it. I can give a thousand excuses for not being able to run 100km, but I know very well the feeling at the finish line is worth trying hard. I very well know how difficult it gets close to the finish line. The last 20km will almost kill me, but if I keep on going, I would be able to fulfill that dream. If I am able to convince my mind that it is achievable, then everything is possible.

Lessons I learned at the Gold Coast Marathon 2017 and the Sydney Marathon 2018.

It is believed that 'a run can change your day and many runs can change your life'. Believing it to be true, running has actually changed my life. I have run several marathons by now and running a marathon for me is as easy and enjoyable as having my favourite food, getting a great sleep or watching a movie. The day I don't hit the treadmill, I feel like I am starving, and I am going to die. Running the Gold Coast Airport Marathon, which is one of the biggest marathons in Australia, was one of my dreams. Running a marathon is not just my passion, my hobby, but also an excuse to travel and meet some extraordinary people.

I was injured in February 2017 while running my last marathon in Mount Dandenong, near Melbourne, but with the grace of God, I recovered in two months. I ran 14 km in the Wings for Life World Run in May 2017 and 2018. This is a unique run where the whole world runs at the same time, any distance before the catcher car catches them. Each runner has to stop as soon as the car passes them. I was able to run around 14 km before the car caught me.

The goal of the Wings for Life Foundation is to raise money around the world to find cure for spinal cord injuries and paraplegia. The race takes place in 34 or 35 countries at the same time.

After finishing this unique race, I was finally ready for the challenge at the Gold Coast. I had just returned from India a day before the Gold Coast marathon and had not been in great form recently. Also, I hardly got time to practice post injury, but since I had registered for it and had a flight ticket, I decided to give it a go. I landed in Gold Coast on the 30th of June 2017, two days before the marathon. As soon as I landed, I went with my friend Devon Lewis to the Gold Coast Convention Centre to collect my bib.

We rested at the Surfers Paradise Backpackers' Hostel. The next day, I went for a practice run in the beach and covered a distance of around 7 km. I rested for the day and certainly got the confidence that I can make it, although my timings were not expected to be as good as my last marathon of 4 hours and 4 minutes.

Next day, the race kicked off at 7:20am from South Port, the Central Business District of Gold Coast. There was a lot of excitement among the crowd and I was running with over 27,000 people. I was running with some of the elite runners from Japan, Singapore, Kenya, USA and different parts of the world. In no time, I crossed the Surfers Paradise beach and the Sky Point Observation Deck, the biggest tower in the Gold Coast.

This area was surrounded by holiday apartments and luxurious houses. I ran another 5 km to reach the Broad Beach, another suburb of Gold Coast. The track of this race was one of the most beautiful tracks along the ocean and almost covered every beach in the city. The best part of this marathon was the volunteers and the motivators and the people of this city.

People who lived along the racetrack came out of their houses and were cheering for their loved ones and even strangers like me by calling their names from the bib. I simply loved it when several strangers said, 'go Suki', I felt more confident about finishing this race. I came across so many friendly residents of this magnificent city, some even offered me watermelon and candy. Soon, I crossed the Miami beach, which actually looked like

Miami of the United States, and a group of choristers was singing and motivating the runners.

The next 5 km was towards Burleigh waters, another suburb with a population of around 13,000. We took a U-turn from here and headed back to the same track and reached the starting point of the race. Till now, I had covered 32km, and I was glad that my destination was only 10 km away. I planned to finish this marathon in under 5 hours, so I tried to speed up a little. From Southport, we headed to Labrador and the Biggera waters before returning back. It was almost 37 km by now. I rested for a minute to drink water and didn't stopped again till the finish line.

As we reached the finish line, people were cheering all over and I felt so good and proud that I finished this race in 4 hours 42 minutes without any proper training. During the marathon, I also got the privilege to meet a great Australian marathon runner Brendan Davies, who finished the race in 2 hours 30 minutes approximately.

This marathon ended, but I am sure many more races are waiting for me. The moral of this story for me was that it is only a mind game as far as running is concerned. Every marathon I run, I also test my endurance and my limits, I always test myself how far I can go. It is believed that human mind is capable of achieving limitless things and we don't even use more than three percent of our brains.

Running for me is not only a sport but also a lifestyle. It helps me stay focused and listen to my inner voice. Finally, I got to run various other marathons after the Gold Coast marathon, like Melbourne and Sydney marathons.

On September 16, 2018, at 7am, at Milsons Point, Sydney, I was joined by over 35,000 runners at the Blackmores Sydney Marathon, and I was there to test my limits. I was able to join some everyday runners and some elite runners from Uganda, USA, Ethiopia, Morocco, Kenya, Australia and around the world and they were able to raise $1,312,292 for various charities.

I was one among the many runners who took part in the 42.195km challenge in order to drain myself physically and mentally and then see what kind of decisions I would make. I wanted to test my physical and mental limits and come out of my comfort zone. In fact, I had told my friends in Melbourne that either I would finish the race in my desired time, or I would die trying.

Yes, I was high on something. Running is a drug to me, and I am proud to be addicted to it. I like running because exhausting myself is the most relaxing moment for me. Running is not only therapeutic but also an awful tasting medicine which helps me recover from any kind of mental and physical illness.

It was one of my dreams to run the Sydney Marathon, but I had no idea I would be joined by such amazing runners from around the world, who were able to finish the marathon in a record time.

I met various runners, who had signed up to become the Guinness World Record holder title, which included fastest marathon dressed as a French maid or one wearing a Malaysian Flag gown. But the most unfeigned moment for me in the marathon was when I saw a father from Queensland, Cameron, running along with his nine-year-old son Aedan in his wheelchair. It was a jaw dropping and an inspiring moment for me, when I heard Aedan's story, who is a nine-year-old boy who cannot stand without assistance or walk without aids. Cameron informed me that Aedan has Cerebral Palsy with low vision and intellectual impairment, and his team is raising money through this marathon.

Immediately, what struck my mind was that if Aedan can finish a marathon with the help of his dad with such disability, what is stopping us all from starting to run? Among all the people I met during the marathon, everyone had a story. Some were running for fitness, some were running because they were addicted like me, some were running to raise money for various charities, while some were there to just have some fun and a good time.

I definitely was able to raise some money for various charities, but I was more into exploring the world's second most expensive city. I did explore this magnificent city by running the marathon. We started at Milsons Point, and in no time, crossed the Sydney Harbour bridge. Later on, we moved towards the Royal Botanic Gardens and was able to reach the Sydney Cricket Ground, passing Hyde Park and Flinders Street. We ended up taking repeated rounds and rounds of Centennial Park. The distance between the starting point (Milsons Point) and the finish point (Sydney Opera House) is hardly 10 km but the track was deliberately made with twists and turns to make it a distance of 42km and it was also to test the patience of every runner. I was losing my patience and was not expecting the track to be curvy.

To be honest, running up the hills is hard work and each incline made my quads hurt and would test my limits. It reminded me of the nightmare in the Himalayas, when I ran 70km ultra marathon. It sounds crazy, but yes, running in the hills is another class and one needs to train hard in order to avoid any injury.

Anyways, in any marathon, the last 5 to 10km are the toughest. It's even harder if you are running alone. My trick for the last leg of the marathon is to start talking to random runners and start motivating them. Once you motivate them, they will also motivate you back at a later stage. When someone tells you 'you got this mate', at this stage of marathon, it acts like an instant energy capsule and motivates me to keep going.

After nearly 5 hours of running, I was able to reach the finishing point, the Sydney Opera House, and the people congratulating and motivating me on the way made me feel so proud. I couldn't wait to share my pics with an iconic medal on social media. While I was boasting on social media about finishing this marathon in 5 hours and 4 minutes, someone in some part of the world, on the same day, made a world record of winning a marathon in 2 hours, 1 minute and 39 seconds. Yes, I am talking about Eliud Kipchoge, who broke the previous world record by winning the Berlin Marathon, 2018.

I could learn a lot from such elite runners on how to improve my timings. This was only one of the marathons I did in the past, and my message to people around the world is that there is no limit to what you can achieve in life. Eliud is an example, and we all can become a better human being, a better decision maker and a better team player by running.

Running Melbourne Marathon thrice taught me that it's a long process, but quitting won't speed it up.

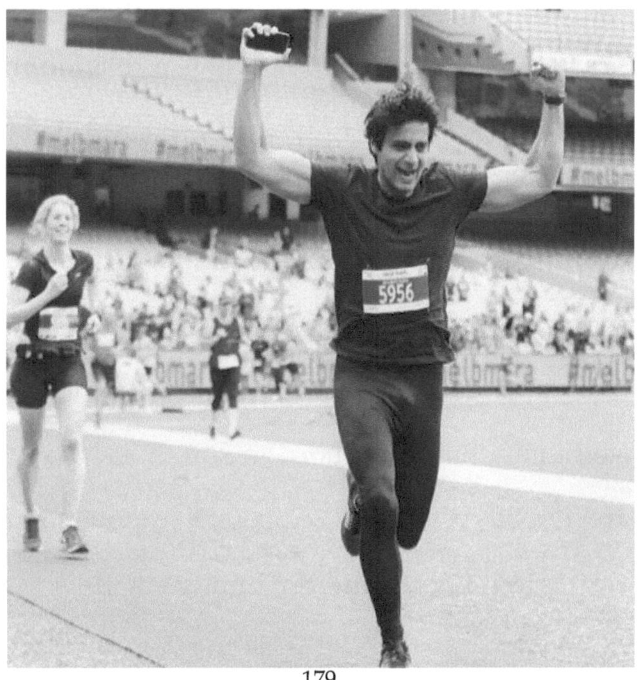

The Melbourne Marathon, 2016.

Apart from the Gold Coast and Sydney marathons, I got the opportunity to run the Melbourne Marathon three times. I came to Melbourne as an overseas student doing my Masters In International Relations and pursuing my passion in media and communications. But since Melbourne is one of the most sporty cities, I had to run the marathon which starts from the Melbourne Cricket Ground (MCG). Sports is a religion in Melbourne, whether it's footy, cricket or marathons.

Every sport is given equal importance and people give lot of respect to sportsperson. I was never good at any sports, but I also very well knew that I am born to run. Every day I dream of becoming a better runner and improving my marathon timings. I finished

Melbourne Marathon in 2016 in 4 hours and 4 minutes. This was one of my best times, but I wish to finish one day in 3 hours. In 2017 and 2018, I also finished the marathon around 4 hours, but both these times it took me more than 4 hours and 10 minutes.

I realised that I had been eating a lot lately in 2017 and 2018, which affected my times. In 2016, I was very much excited about my first marathon in Australia and I remember starting the race outside the MCG at Batman Avenue. We headed north along Batman Avenue and turned left into Flinders Street, an iconic Melbourne train station, and then headed along the St Kilda Road.

At St Kilda Junction, we turned right into Fitzroy Street then right into Lakeside Drive and did a lap in an anti-clockwise circuit of the Lake. We crossed Albert Park and covered the whole of St. Kilda road with lot of twists and turns, and finally returned back to the MCG. The cut off times for the runners was 5 hours and 30 minutes, but I was able to finish easily much before that in all three years.

Running the Mumbai Marathon, 2016 & the Bangalore Ultra Marathon, 2011, taught me to try and fail as most people don't even try.

Like Sydney, Melbourne and Gold Coast, the Mumbai and Bangalore marathons will always be in my heart. Mumbai is a beautiful city. It is the entertainment and financial capital of India and running along with some Bollywood stars and business leaders was a terrific experience. I remember the then brand ambassador of the Standard Chartered Mumbai Marathon, 2016 and my favourite Bollywood actor, John Abraham was hosting the flag for the marathon at the starting point of the race.

5:39am, January 17th, 2016, a minute before the marathon kicked off, I was giving a byte to New Delhi Television, telling the English news channel how excited I was to run my first full Mumbai Marathon. 5:40am came and I finally started running with over 40,000 people, some of whom came from across the world. It was still dark, and the weather was pleasant enough to make my run an enjoyable one. I was very much confident that I would finish the 42.195km run since I had done my homework well. I ran 36 km at Delhi's Lodhi Garden, a day before I landed in Mumbai. So, I was very much confident that I would finish my run, but the big question was whether I could finish under the target time of 4 hours.

We all started from the Chhatrapati Shivaji Terminus and ran towards the Oberoi and Trident Hotel, passing the Church Gate Station. One of the most beautiful things about the Mumbai Marathon is the track. The track is so beautiful and running by the Arabian sea made my run even more delightful. During the first two hours of my race, I took no breaks, as I knew I had to utilise my full energy to cover the maximum distance I could. I passed through Wankhede stadium, Chowpatty, the Haji Ali, and I was enjoying each and every moment of my run.

Finally, we reached the Bandra-worli sea link. Running at the sea link was an incredible experience. It reminded me of the half marathon I ran in 2014. I had passed the same bridge with a magnificent view. The best thing about the marathon was the volunteers,

Mumbaikars (residents of Mumbai), and the Mumbai Police.

People, including children, came out from their houses and were encouraging runners with motivational placards on their hands. In fact, children as young as 5-years-old were offering me oranges, chocolates and water. But the thing which surprised me the most was the Mumbai Police. They were all over the track to protect us from any unforeseen contingencies but at the same time, they were also motivating the runners. I heard a policeman saying, 'C'mon you can do it'.

I had run the Delhi and Bangalore Marathon as well in India, but never had the experience of seeing such amazing people. It was love at first sight with Mumbai for me. It is said that Mumbai is a city of dreams, a financial and entertainment capital, but it is also one of my hometowns now. And yes, people don't stare at women in Mumbai even if they are wearing a mini, which I felt Delhiites need to learn from.

I had completed 21 km in less than 2 hours. I passed Antilla, one of the most expensive houses in the world, Lilavati hospital, and Siddhivinayak temple. I was carrying some coffee packs, which I dug into with water during my 30 second breaks. It gave me some instant energy. Yes, now my pace was getting slow, but seeing thousands of people running along with me, I automatically got the energy. I was passing the same track again and had crossed the 36km mark. It was 9 o'clock and I was hopeful of finishing my run within the next 30 minutes.

I had a nine-to-five job in Delhi and taking time off for running in the extreme hot and cold weather of Delhi made me feel crazy. But yes, I do run on treadmill every time I hit the gym and people stare at me thinking I am crazy to run so fast. I had practiced, but yes, I could have done much better with my times.

I finished the marathon in exactly 4 hours 8 minutes, but the dream is to finish a marathon in 3 hours in order to qualify for Boston Marathon. Yes, every marathoner's dream is to run the Boston, but I am sure one day I will qualify and have financial support, and my dream would be fulfilled.

My first ultra marathon (50km) in Bangalore,

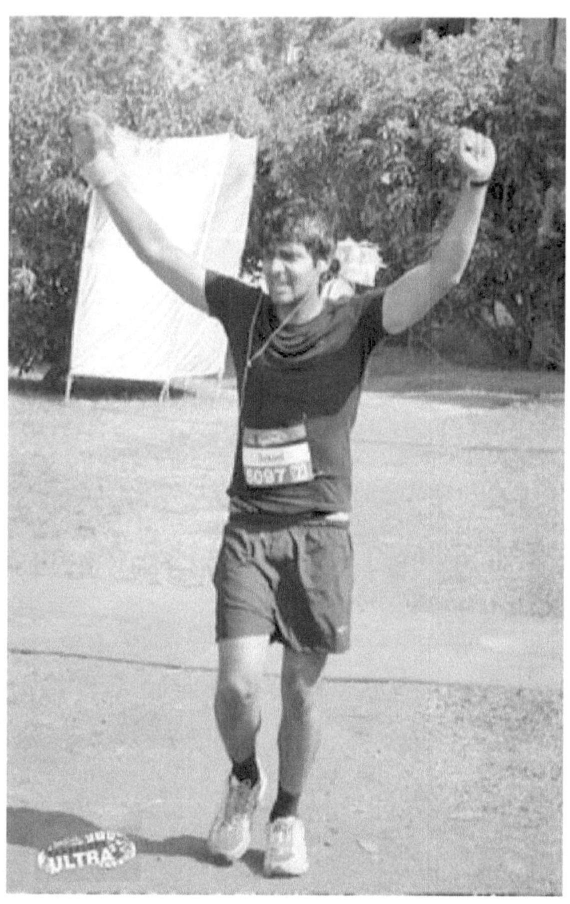

India, which I finished in nearly 8 hours in 2011.

I will also never forget my first Ultra Marathon in Southern India. I ran the Bangalore Ultra Marathon in 2011 in nearly 8 hours. It was a very proud moment for me. I was very young, around 22 years of age. I remember having very bad rashes on my legs afterwards, as I didn't have proper shoes and leggings to run a marathon.

I generally recommend not wearing underwear, but tights, which prevents any rashes on thighs. I was barely able to walk for few days after the run. I remember getting completely tanned in the sun after running for 8 hours. I never applied sunscreen. The feeling at the finish line was terrific.

I also remember calling my dad after the run and he told me a story about the race and how to never look back but keep moving forward. I have no idea who told me to register for this event but somehow, I came across an advertisement for Runners for Life and I registered for the event. The Bangalore Ultra is part of Runners for Life, an organisation dedicated to increase the population of runners in India. It is one of the largest running communities in India and aims to conduct multiple activities to expand its community. Thus, the most important lesson I have absorbed by running these marathons is that human mind can achieve limitless things. We just need to be focused and keep trying hard.

Himalayan Adventures

One of the biggest adventures of my life was running 70km, or 43 miles, in the Himalayas. I had registered for this event called 70km 'GET SET RUNN – Tuffman Shimla Ultra 2.0', without knowing how painful it would be to run in the mountains. But to be honest, the pain you undergo while running long distances is nothing to the feeling of joy or epic satisfaction at the finish line.

I realised everything I ever wanted to know about myself could be learned by running 70km. I just wanted to be successful in my goal of completing this ultra marathon.

Over a few years, since I had begun running marathons, I realised that there is no difference between running and being successful in life. When somebody gives all their potential in achieving their goal, it changes their life and the lives of others who consider them an inspiration. I consider every marathon as being successful or unsuccessful. One can see, in the eyes of a runner, what he or she is aiming for and how they feel after finishing the race in their desired time.

When I started running, I didn't care much about my times. For me, just finishing a marathon was more than enough to get a good night sleep. But when I started getting positive feedback from people on social media, I started taking this hobby seriously and now I train to finish races in my desired time. I redesigned my brain to be able to complete the race in my expected time. We all undergo a tremendous amount of pressure to be able to perform well, whether it's our marathon, career, relationship or health. As I am running, I always feel that I cannot afford to make many mistakes.

One short break at the water station could lower my pace and decrease the flow of my run. Running for me is like climbing mountains or an adventure sport. It is also teamwork. We need to keep motivating other runners and run like a team. I do not feel that other runners are my competitors, but that they are my mates with whom I need to collaborate.

I feel that when I am running, I need to show my full capacity, the expectations from people I know like my friends, family and even strangers are very high, so I have to use my full potential and be able to work under pressure. I need to run with strength and show kindness to other runners. We humans are always greedy and want more in our lives. But I realised that I am not in a rat race, but I want to run along with thousands of other runners. The single most important fact is that I could not have been able to run 70km alone. So, we all need someone in our lives to help us become the best version of ourselves. Also, I feel the joy when I am able to empower others to be able to achieve their goals.

Trust me, when someone finishes an ultra marathon like 60 or 70km, it changes their life. We all just need to be patient and be persistent in this long journey towards success.

Life is definitely a gift and we don't need to waste it. While for some people money might be the reason for their happiness, for me, I am always looking for fulfillment, satisfaction, meaning, and purpose. I get to realise my purpose when I run a marathon. It's the greatest fulfillment of my life. I am able to inspire some of my friends, who can't run even 2km, and show them the importance of physical fitness. I am so grateful to have this unique passion and I am here to make a difference in the lives of others.

It is believed that if you have clothes on your body, a roof over your head, a bed to sleep in and some food to eat, you are richer than 75% of people in this world. We all know that a large number of people around the world have no access to water, food or electricity. We have so many things to be grateful for.

When I am having a bad day in my life, I am complaining that everything around is bad – like, this house is bad, this job is bad, this person is bad, this country is bad, this food is bad, this water is bad. I just think to myself, the world has already so many people to criticise, but what I am doing to make it better? We all are aware that there are major global problems, like climate change, which we are facing today, but what are we doing to make this world a better place?

Instead of complaining, if we all start thinking of thousands of children working in Mica mines in India, who are paid less than 1 dollar a day and have no access to education, we would probably complain less of our lives. I think of the mines in South Africa, where labourers are working in some of the most inhumane conditions in diamond mines at 43 degree Celsius, who are underpaid and only get to see their family once a year.

We all need to be grateful if our lives are better than those workers. Running has also taught me to practice gratitude. I am not happy because of running but I am happier because when I see that me running long distance can bring joy and happiness into others' lives. Research has proved that we are happier when we share, serve humanity and support one another. We are happier when we give back. It's unfortunate that we are wired for generosity but educated for greed. I run for various charities and some of the great causes I have run for are for cancer patients, indigenous peoples of the world, refugees and climate change. I am just trying to give back to the world by running.

Mind matters: how I prepared my mind to run 70km.

While it's my dream to run beyond human limits one day, I believe that meditation and preparing our mind is the key. I always grew up being connected to nature, mountains, seas and forests. As long as I am in nature, I feel like I am in my element. As a teenager, I always use to escape to the mountains, and my family use to think I was crazy. They used to call me an escapist. But actually, I was not escaping from the problems, I was just being myself. Similarly, I am not running away from my problems, but I am running to solve many problems. I love the smell of nature, especially after it rains, and I am able to connect with nature. When the mountains are calling, I have to go. I do love hiking and trekking but running is definitely my first love. But if you are running in the mountains, it's very much similar to hiking as we cannot run the whole of a long distance which is around 1800m above sea level.

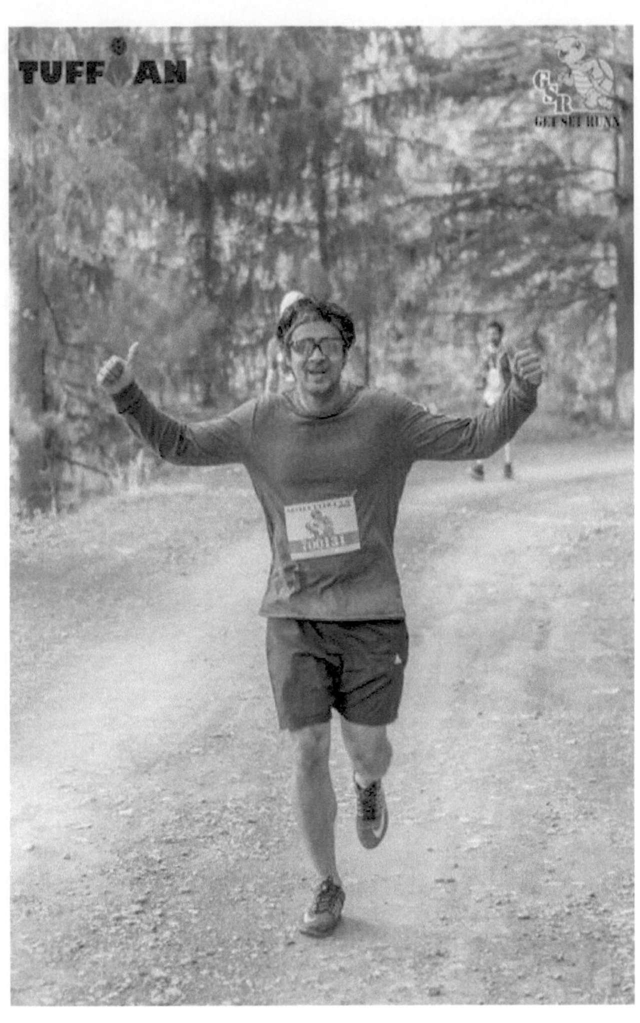

Shimla Ultra Marathon 70km in the Himalayas, I finished it in nearly 13 hours in 2016.

On June 18, 2016, at 4am, I woke up with a great determination. By 10pm that night, I went to bed with an epic satisfaction. Yes, I had registered for the 70km 'GET SET RUNN-Tuffman Shimla Ultra 2.0' and as a journalist was also covering the event. I registered for such an event as I realised that it was time for me to dare to endure and get out of my comfort zone. The race kicked off at 5.45am and there were around 45 athletes in my category.

At an average elevation of 2,146m, the racetrack at Mashobra, a town in Shimla district of Himachal Pradesh, was amazingly beautiful. We started with 2km of elevation, followed by plains and some 12km of descent. I was very much at ease in finishing the first lap of 35kms in about five hours. The pleasant weather also added to my running ecstasy.

But the real test began in the second lap when my legs almost gave up 17kms away from the finish line. One really needs strong willpower and determination. It is said that your body can stand almost anything, but it's your mind that you have to convince. The same was the case with me, I was able to convince my mind to shove my body and that made all the difference. I had made up my mind that whether I walked, jogged, ran or crawled, I had to finish the race.

I remember chanting the Tibetan Mantra 'Om Mani Padme Hum', praying for some energy. I was eagerly waiting for the next water station and the finishing line. I also met many runners on the way who gave me hi-fives and motivated me to finish the race. The biggest inspiration of all the runners were Col. Saurabh Singh Shekhawat, (Army officer who has conquered Mt. Everest thrice) and Delhi-based International ultra marathon runner Arun Bhardwaj. Being an amateur runner, I felt so privileged to run with them.

In fact, if I go back to my running story, it all started when I was 14 years old. In school I use to play basketball, football, and used to love goal keeping. But one can say I was jack of all trades and master of none. In simple words, I was not good professionally at any sports. I always wanted to be involved in sports as it teaches you lot of things in life.

So, I used to run a lot, religiously, every evening, sometimes alone, sometimes with a running buddy. Slowly, I started taking part in marathons while in college, and my latest run was the Standard Chartered Mumbai Marathon in January which I finished in 4 hour 8 minutes.

But, running in the mountains was a completely different story. I have one piece of advice for people planning to run a marathon. We should run from our heart and mind rather than our feet. To be honest, I had a nine-to-five job in Delhi as a journalist, and taking time off for running in the extreme hot and cold weather of the city made me feel crazy. But yes, I do run on treadmill every time I hit the gym and people stare at me, thinking I am crazy to run so fast.

I had practiced for a month at Delhi's Nehru Park, running sometimes 10km and sometimes up to 38km, but it is always better to practice in the mountains for such a marathon.

So, I finally crossed the finish line of this ultra marathon in exactly 12 hours 58 minutes (two minutes ahead of cut-off time of 13 hours). The feeling was epic, I felt like I was about to reach Everest, or I had already reached the summit. Also, people congratulating me made me feel on top of the world.

I am not hoping to change the world or India overnight with my runs, but yes, perhaps, someone once inspired me, and I am here to inspire others. I just want to give the message to people around that yes, one person can make a difference and there is no limit to what you can achieve in life.

My friends or family may think I am a lunatic for running such distances, or a crazy person for scaling mountains, but it's imperative to chase one's passion and dreams. And most important of all, the challenge to run such distances in the mountains motivates you and tests your endurance level.

It also made me realise who I am and what I am capable of.

What is the significance of *Om Mani Padme Hun* in my life? It gives me energy.

While running this ultra marathon, I changed my perspective towards life. I realised that the world might have several problems, but I am one of the solutions to the problem. I acknowledged that the universal mind has solutions to all my problems.

I learned that if I don't heal the pain of my past then I will suffer all over again in my future. And I became more positive by understanding the power of Buddhism. The Dalai Lama teaches some significant lessons of life and I truly follow him. As a child I often use to visit Dharamasala, a small city in the Indian Himalayas and home to the Dalai Lama and the Tibetan government in exile.

I was attracted to the peace and chants of Tibetan Mantras (a thought behind a speech or action) and the Buddhist prayer, 'Om Mani Padme Hum'. I often try to meditate for five to ten minutes, chanting the prayer, when I am seeking some help or suffering from anxiety. It does help me. And to be honest, nobody had told me about this prayer, but I was attracted to it by myself during my several visits to Dharamsala.

I do practice chanting this prayer either sitting or lying down or playing it on YouTube with my table lamp on in my room. Practicing this mantra silently in our minds could really have powerful impacts. Whenever I lack some power or energy during long distance running, I do chant this prayer silently and I do feel empowered. This mantra seeks to cultivate and spread compassion and love.

It also helps me overcome any kind of stress. Running has taught me to have dangerous dreams. In Marine, there is a saying, that everyone wants to go to heaven, but nobody wants to die. 99% of people who wants to be successful or a movie star or have a ripped six pack body, are not willing to go through the sacrifices in order to accomplish their dreams. For example, convincing our minds to choose actions which are in our own best interest. What do we eat, what time do we get up, what time do we go to bed, what kind of people do we surround ourselves with?

These are small steps to self-discipline, which a runner needs to undergo. Self-discipline is the key to all material success.

There is a saying that you cannot win the war against the world if you can't win against your own mind. Every time I run, I feel like I am fighting war against my mind. My mind is always telling me to eat unhealthily, sleep till late and have a hedonistic lifestyle. But if I am able to control my mind with self-discipline, I can win the world. The hard part is not to get my body in shape but to get my mind in shape. If I am able to tell my mind to eat healthy, I will always be in shape. I feel my body is a temple, which I need to maintain in a healthy state.

Every time I hit the gym; I love running on the treadmill. I love these words from Will Smith, who said: 'The only thing that I see that is distinctly different about me is I am not afraid to die on a treadmill. I will not be out-worked, period. You might have more talent than me, you might be smarter than me, you might be sexier than me, you might be all of those things. You got me in nine categories, but if we get on the treadmill together, there's two things: You are getting off first or I am going to die. It's really that simple.'

Every time I listen to these words I could easily connect. I call myself a treadmill addict. I love running on a treadmill and it helps me realise my full potential. I feel really confident running on the treadmill for two to three hours. Although some people do not recommend treadmill for marathon runners, I personally do enjoy my time on treadmill. Treadmill running also helps me overcome any kind of fear of failure. Also, I am just being myself when I am on a treadmill.

Running on a treadmill for long hours makes me realise that it's ok if we all have some dangerous dreams. Motivational speaker and author Wayne Dyer had said, 'When you change the way you look at things, the things you look at change.' I absolutely love this quote as when we see failure as a pathway to success, when I see rejection as redirection, when I see things differently or from a different perspective, it adds positivity to my life. I run, not because I want to punish myself, but because it makes me realise my full potential. In fact, we all have some unique spark within us, that makes us different.

No matter how life will treat us, we should never lose hope and always aim to reach the finish line. Our journey will be full of challenges and obstacles, but we should have the courage to have dangerous dreams. By dangerous dreams, I mean courage to follow our heart and passion.

Many people, including my friends and family are making this mistake today as they live by other people's thinking. They always think of what other people will think, and many dreams are killed. If I start listening to other people's thinking, I would have never been able to live my life or run even a single marathon. It is ok to have different and unique dreams. People who have always chosen a different path have changed the world. I love what Steve Jobs said, 'We have to find what we love.' And secondly, being consistent is the key to success. I do not aspire to just be able to pay my bills and rent, but I aim to make a difference in the world. If we have to suffer in order to be great, why not.

How we all can overcome stress by running.

We all are facing some stress today as we compare ourselves with others. We are trapped by insecurities. We live in a world today when our choices of life can completely change in a moment. Life can change in a minute if we lose someone we love, our family or partner, lose our job or savings. We can also lose our house, our car, in a natural disaster. Our marriages can end, health issues can appear, and we can have job losses due to economic collapse. This is a very common feature of the modern world we live in today. So how do we cope with modern day challenges? I always believe that we have to pursue our passion and hobbies to overcome stress.

For me, running is a hobby, which makes me the best version of myself. No matter how many material things I acquire, I will not be happy if I am not doing things which I am passionate about or things I love. There is a saying that if we get up every morning and don't do the things that make our heart sing, we will feel an overwhelming sense of regret when we are lying on our death beds. I personally love working out in the gym and the day I miss it, I feel a sense of discomfort. I am sure many people feel the same. We have to do something we love every week, if not every day. Running ultra marathons is an expensive sport. Sometimes I am not able to afford to register for a race. But then I feel that if I could save a little to pursue this passion, it would help me live with a purpose.

I will eventually become frustrated, listless and completely devoid of a purpose for existence, if I am not able to run or live a meaningful life. I always believe life is very short and very few people in this planet get to live a meaningful life.

It is only about grabbing every opportunity next to you and experiencing every possible adventure. The fear of failure stops us from doing a lot of things, but I have never feared failure. I do not want to have regrets by the time I turn 60 or 70 for not doing the things I loved. Many people call me crazy or a lunatic for running such long distances, but I feel it's imperative to pursue one's dream. True happiness comes from fulfilling your dreams and at end of my life, I do not want to repent for not being able to do what I love.

Mountaineering is another sport which fascinates me a lot. One of my favourite role models is Bear Grylls, as far as adventurous sports or mountaineering is concerned. I grew up watching him on one of the most watched shows on the planet – Man vs Wild on the discovery channel, and I was able to resonate with it.

There are a lot of life lessons which could be learned from the program. I have also learned various life lesson while running and climbing mountains. Running at the Shimla Ultra marathon was one of the best adventures I had in the mountains. But I also do have a passion for hiking and scuba diving. I remember it was July 2012, when I decided to go for an expedition in Leh, India. At a height of 4900m/nearly 16,000ft above sea level, I still cannot forget the day I was struggling in the cold region of Rumbak village in Leh-Ladakh.

I was tossing and turning whole night in the homestay, praying to get some sleep but my condition deteriorated due to the extreme cold weather. Memories are still fresh in my mind of the Stok La trek in July 2012 with my guide and some foreign tourist. That night, as the sun disappeared, I experienced a new sort of cold wind, one I never experienced before. It was deeper and seemed to penetrate through my blanket. My nose was running, and I felt the snot freeze as it dangled from my nostril. I felt awful as headache and cold was not letting me sleep. And besides that, I had not eaten much for dinner. I had Ladakhi tea which was a bit salty and some wai-wai noodles which I was carrying in my rucksack. My guide had no problem in acclimatization in the village as he was a local and use to make such trips very often.

The best solution for the discomfort was to numb the mind and lie in haze. I also remember using the traditional toilet in the village where there was no water or tissue paper and I had to use mud to wash my hands. Next day, I woke up early as I managed to get an hour sleep somehow. It was 6am and I could see in the pre-dawn glow. I wore my jacket and sneaked out for a walk around the village. I felt I was in one of the most beautiful part of the country. After that, I huddled back into the homestay where I was offered tea by the local family who lived there. My guide and I held warm mugs of tea close to us and sipped noisily.

Though I was not well enough to move ahead to conquer the Stok la peak, I never gave up. We decided to move to higher altitude slowly and said good-bye to the Ladakhi family and thanked them for their hospitality. The sun was still low in the sky when we moved ahead and never looked back. As the morning progressed, we snaked our way tentatively across the higher altitude.

Despite the slow pace, the altitude meant that we were soon tired. Also, I was facing breathing problems as I was hardly getting any oxygen. Soon, we found ourselves climbing methodically and slowly up near the Stok la peak. The excitement welled up and I felt so strong seeing our mission from so close. Also, how can I forget the English guy I met somewhere before the peak, who gave me tips of climbing mountains. He also taught me a funny trick to find our way when we get lost in the mountains – the 'stomachache theory', as he said. He truly believed that if one goes the wrong way in the mountains, the person gets some stomachache.

At 1pm we finally reached the peak and lit a bonfire. The feeling of being able to reach such a height was amazing. My confidence was so high, and I remembered what my dad usually advised me, to always look in front and never give up. I thanked God for everything and at the same time this was not the end of me, as now I was dreaming of going to Everest base camp in Nepal. I always had this burning desire to go higher, and I longed to witness the summit of Everest.

We met some guys from Poland while retreating and rested for some time. I had nothing left to eat and neither did my guide, so we shared some omelettes from the Polish people we met.

As we descended through the valley, our bodies enjoyed richer air. During this trek, I had proved that I can cope at this altitude and survive. At 4pm, I breathed deeply at the top of the icefall as I gazed down into the depths below. The more I saw it, the more I thought of going back in. As we squatted, I saw another village, which indicated that we were not far from reaching the trekkers' point.

I never realised, but it started drizzling and it got more tough for us to descend as it was slippery. A slight mistake would have cost us our lives. Slowly and slowly we were moving downwards, and at around 6pm when it was almost dark, I reached the city of Leh. I met my uncle and hugged him as he was desperately waiting for me to come down to the city. He was not able to contact me during my trek as my phone was unreachable. I shared my wonderful experience with my uncle, and we had lovely dinner in a German bakery that night.

This was only my third trek in India but mountaineering and running has always been my passion. This small trek will be always special in my life and I hope I conquer the Everest someday. Just like running, mountaineering is also my passion. I love nature and adventures and I am able to connect with it so much. It is so much a part of me when I am in nature. No amount of money, big house, big car, or job status could give me happiness as much as being in nature and experiencing it.

I do love travelling as well, as it makes me more compassionate and a great learner. My family never liked me going to the mountains or doing something adventurous. According to them, being successful is having job status, power, money and getting married, having kids and then waiting for your retirement or death, whichever comes first. But I always consider being successful as pursuing your passion, being healthy, giving back to the world and the society.

Hiking in the mountains have taught me a way to live life, to never give up, to make crucial life and career decisions. It has prepared me to face challenges. It was exactly three years, since, I conquered the Stok la peak at 4900m above sea level in Leh, I decided to go for the Stok Kangri expedition at 6100m above sea level: a challenging one indeed. It was June 8, 2015, and I landed in Srinagar, the summer capital of Jammu and Kashmir. Yes, it was indeed paradise on earth. To be honest, I was a bit intimidated with media reports hovering my mind of escalating violence across LoC, which also made me a suspicious man. Yes, there were army bunkers every 100m in the streets of Srinagar, but I cannot deny the fact that it was paradise on earth.

I took a taxi from the airport to TRC (Tourist Reservation Centre) and my driver, named Aashiq, briefed me about the places to explore in the city. I had one complete day to spend in Srinagar and I decided to go for a Shikara ride. The Shikara is a type of wooden boat found on Dal Lake in Srinagar and is one of the most soothing, relaxing and romantic rides. In fact, lot of Bollywood movies have been shot in these Shikaras. The boat rider told me to lie down and act like a king. I was enjoying my ride and an ice-cream seller approached us in another shikara. Yes, it was a typical kashmiri ice-cream named 'gulbadan'. I simply loved it.

The two-hour ride was over in no time and yes, I was roaming in the markets near the Dal

Lake. I came across several bikers who were riding the Royal Enfield and were on their way to Leh from Kanya Kumari, the southernmost part of India. The next morning, I woke up at 5am, with an excitement to move ahead to Leh. I had booked a shared taxi and within 12 hours, I was in "incredible Ladakh". I was supposed to stay at my friend Omyer Lassu's house.

I had no idea that my school buddy's father was such a popular politician in Leh. In fact, as soon as I said Lassu to any taxi driver, everyone was willing to drop me at my friend's residence. I spent two nights at Lassu's before heading out for the expedition. The incredible cook named Ali made the best dishes of mutton and chicken for me. I felt so honoured and lucky at the same time. On day three in Leh, after proper acclimatisation, I started my expedition with my guide Aamta.

It was four to five hours walk from Chang Ma in Leh to the Mankorma camp site. Mankorma is at an altitude of 14,200 ft, and is a stunning site to observe. I rested in Mankorma for a night before heading to base camp at 16,300 ft (5000m) above sea level. I was not getting sleep and was tossing and turning the whole night inside my sleeping bag in the tent. On day six, I met a new guide who had more professional knowledge of mountains. My new guide told me that we will be heading to the summit at midnight and back to base camp by early morning.

Only two people had made it to the summit this season. I was cold and was trying to acclimatise as much as I could. That night at the base camp, I also met group of students and teachers from an international school in Pune. We were at a height of around 5,000m and even going to toilet in the open was a challenge for me. Being one of biggest fan of Bear Grylls, I was enjoying each and every moment of it instead of complaining. "Failing is not a crime, Lack of effort is" and I was all ready for it. Patience on the mountains, especially on this Stok Kangri expedition is the key to climbing successfully. It is one of the reasons that most climbers tend to be older.

They have more of it which I lacked. Ultimately it is the mountain who say whether you can climb or not. We are but pawns in this game, the decisions all lie with the mountains. That night I was awake at 1 am for the summit but then my body did not permit me to move ahead. In the morning, we tried again and reached till 5,200 m. It was snowing heavily. My mind was not ready to give up. I took a decision to retreat, as I was literally frozen and was also short of oxygen.

We crouched and watched as the cloud of snow settled only a few hundred feet away. As we squatted, we could see Base camp clearly below. Binoculars would be watching us from there. By two in the afternoon, we were gazing back up at the now-silent icefall. We headed back to Leh with a beautiful memory and a hope to conquer the peak someday, it was good to be back. The next adventure was in Australia. I moved to Australia in 2016 to study International Relations and Media and communication. I was really passionate about what I was studying but I realised travelling and exploring this magnificent country could help me learn a lot more than in classrooms. I decided to go scuba diving with my best mate at the Great Barrier Reef in my summer break.

I thought to myself you live once, so why not do what you were born to do! In fact, everyone has a bucket-list written in their personal diary which perhaps they want to strike off before they die. Being the adventurous person I am, scuba diving and sky diving which are challenging sports, were always at the brim of my bucket-list. So I could not have asked for more as I landed at nature's biggest gift to Australia, the Great Barrier Reef in Cairns, Queensland. Myself and my friend Hui Dong had saved some money from our part time jobs and decided to do this adventure. It was the most beautiful thing I had ever experienced in my life. I was in a different world all together with fish all around, complemented by coral reefs. Scuba diving is an adventurous sport which also tests your limits.

To be honest, being a first-time diver, I was a bit nervous. I am not a great swimmer either. But then, growing up on 'Man Vs Wild' and being a big fan of British adventurer Bear Grylls, I couldn't but do it. "Bravery is about facing up to the things we fear the most, and overcoming and conquering those fears," someone rightly said. And I was in the middle of the Pacific Ocean testing my limits.

For those like me who are first timers, I would only suggest that there is only one rule of diving: to 'equalize'. Now, what is equalize? It perhaps took me one unsuccessful dive or a couple of hours to understand that. I went almost 10- meter deep inside the ocean, of course with the swimsuit and oxygen mask and other equipment, but my ear started hurting.

My instructor Irene told me I can't dive any more as I was not being able to equalize. I got tad worried as I had come all the way from Melbourne just to dive. But then, my instructor taught me the right method and I tried again. Equalize means when you swallow, your soft palate muscles pull your Eustachian tubes open, allowing air to rush from your throat to your middle ears and equalize the pressure. That's the faint "pop" or "click" you hear about every other swallow. In simple terms to equalize means to close your nose with your fingers and try to pump air out from your ears. It will make a pop up. This is the simplest definition of equalizing. So finally, I made it to the reef. I was one lucky person to see the United Nations world heritage site,

Great Barrier Reef. I observed amazing varieties of fish, Jellyfish, tortoise and some divers were also fortunate enough to see baby sharks. Before the diving, we had done snorkelling, so I felt quite confident inside the water. After 40 minutes of diving and 20 minutes of snorkelling we were back onboard the 'Passion Paradise', one of the best cruises from Cairns to the Great Barrier Reef. I dived almost 10 meters deep in the ocean and beheld the coral reef.

I felt I was alive like a fish and there was a reason to it. The cruise had amazing diving instructors like Nick, Denis and Irene to name a few, who were so friendly and made me very comfortable inside the water. Before diving we were also given instructions like how to use underwater sign marks to talk to your instructors. It reminded me of the

Bollywood movie 'Zindagi Na Milegi Dobara', where Katrina Kaif, the actress helps superstar Hrithik Roshan dive and teaches how to use sign marks under water.

Nick also suggested me to do a pro diving 5-day course which probably I decided to do it in my next trip to Cairns. Later on, after having a lovely lunch we moved to our next location which was Michaelmas Cay Island. It was one of the most beautiful things on earth. I loved the island with birds chirping all over.

We met two girls from Canada, who were onboard with us, one of them was Helena. We went snorkeling again with our diving instructor Denis. This reef was in fact more beautiful and my friend Hui Dong didn't hesitate in taking underwater photos from his Go pro. On the way back to Cairns, we had coffee and some biscuits onboard passion of paradise, where I met people from different places including Canada, Italy, Scotland and the UK, who had come to see one of the most beautiful things on earth.

Great Barrier Reef is unfortunately dying due to climate change. In fact, scientists have predicted that in the next 50 years there would be no reef alive. Teams of researchers from James Cook University in Cairns are returning to the same 83 reefs that they surveyed underwater in March 2016 at the height of the bleaching event.

"Millions of corals in the north of the Great Barrier Reef died quickly from heat stress in March and since then, many more have died more slowly," says Dr. Greg Torda, whose team recently returned from re-surveying reefs near Lizard Island.

The Australian Government has certainly a great responsibility to preserve this heritage site which generates millions of revenue through tourism. Anyways, on the way back we were all proud of getting a successful diving certificate from our instructors.

Nick, the diving instructor also held a short presentation talking about the reef and things the government need to do to prevent the reef from extinction. It was 5 pm when we reached Cairns after beautiful nine-hour trip which I would always cherish. We said adios to all the diving instructors and headed back to our backpackers hostel where I cooked lamb curry for dinner to celebrate with my friend Dong.

While there is nothing wrong in pursuing our adventures, hobbies and passion but the biggest lesson I learned was to ensure our safety. Scuba Diving is not recommended for heart patients and people who are overweight. I always ensure that I am with someone I am close to so that we can look after each other.

Pursuing these adventure sports also helps me recover from any kind of stress or anxiety. Of course, these are expensive sports and many people cannot afford to do that. But I always believe if I am able to save up for these life experiences, it would help me live a meaningful life.

I believe that physical fitness and mental fitness is equally important in order to increase our productivity. For me following my passion which is running helps me enhance my productivity. Some people believe that great ideas strike our head when we are in the shower, but for me great ideas come when I am running. Lot of things is going in my head while I am running long distances. I attract positiveness and release toxic people from my life. I believe our thoughts create things and if our thoughts are negative it will lead to negative things. If my thoughts are positive, my words will be positive, and I can use my positive thoughts to create positive things. What did Steve Jobs do to change the world? He had a positive idea and he used that positiveness to create things we use today. I often become negative if I am surrounded by negative people. In today's world, it's very difficult to make true friends as most of us are running after money and consider having money as being successful.

One of the basic things that is instilled in me is that I can never hurt anyone by my words. If someone abuses me and I react and abuse back, I am harming myself. But if I completely ignore and move forward to do productive things which enhances my wellbeing, it would help me in my growth. But that does not mean if somebody ran away with your money or hurt you intentionally, we completely forgive them. It is not easy to move forward sometimes. But when I am running, I am actually trying to move forward and get away from failure, negative thoughts, and poor relationships. When I am running, I am thinking of these words: love, kindness, compassion, helping others, smile, protect environment.

Just imagine if the world starts thinking in this way, there would be no hatred, no jealousy, no anger and we all treat each other with respect. What if all religion, communities, languages, and cultures were treated equally? What if the world united to solve global problems like climate change, water crisis, food crisis, terrorism, mental health? The world would definitely be a better place. Even though politicians might try to divide communities around the world for their vested interest, we could unite ourselves with positivity and by running. Nobody in the world would die of hunger if we all become kind and help each other.

By running long distances, I am just trying to build a community for change. I am just being myself when I am running. Many people do not care whether I run 100km or 1000km, but my close friends always motivate me and consider me as a role model. I do not run because I want more likes on Instagram, but I am running and sending a message at the same time that physical fitness helps me, and it might help my friends as well and change their life for good. We can live with no shell and be ourselves. We don't have to live by other people's thinking. If we are able to find the purpose of life, we would be going to share that purpose with our family, children, parents and friends.

I realised that running is the purpose of my life and these experiences of ultra marathons, mountaineering, travelling, scuba diving could help me maximise my purpose. We are been constantly told to follow a monotonous life as we fear innovation and change. But the world needs more entrepreneurs, CEOs, leaders in sports, politics, entertainment and business.

Running has taught me another important lesson that we live in a world today where there is so much hate, so we need to spread love and affection to people around us. Long distance running helps me test my endurance level and makes me realise that consistency is the key. But consistency only comes with discipline. Discipline is the bridge between goals and accomplishment and in order to achieve any target, we need to have a disciplined life. Discipline starts with getting up early, making our bed and going for a run on a regular basis. Discipline also starts with controlling our emotions. I do often get angry like other human beings if somebody insults me or abuse me.

We often face confrontation with our boss at workplace, sometimes our political views differ, our perspective towards life differs from our family or friends. Many of my friends and family members consider making money and having big houses and material wealth as success. I consider being healthy, following passion and helping others as being success. My definition of success is different from most of the people I come across. This often leads to confrontation and I get angry. But the best way to let the anger go away is to be compassionate. Running has helped me to not let others opinion about me make me weak.

I believe compassion helps us remain calm. In fact, yoga and meditation also teaches us to be compassionate. Mindfulness can bring hope and decrease our suffering. I do not practice yoga personally, but since I moved to Australia, I realised that yoga has become more popular in the west than in India, where it originated. People are going through a lot of stress in the world we are living today and mindfulness, running, exercise can help us become more compassionate.

I always believe the secret to happiness is our relationship. When my relationship is weak with the person I love, my family, my close friend, I am unhappy. When I say every day to my family that I love them very much and I am always there for them, it improves our relationship. When I am running, I am inspiring people and building positive relationship. It is also a best way to de-stress. I do breathe out for longer than breathing in, in order to overcome stress and of course when I am running. We need to believe today its ok to be not perfect in this world.

All of us are going through a lot of struggles in our life. The most elite athlete in the world, to celebrities and CEOs have suffered from anxiety and depression. When I was suffering from anxiety, I shared my problems with people around me. I realised I am not the only one, but 1 in 4 Victorians in Australia are suffering from anxiety and mental ill-health. The prevalence of mental illness in young people is especially on rise. The World Health Organization has confirmed that depression will overtake heart disease as the number one cause of illness worldwide by 2030.

So, the magnitude of the problem is huge, and we are yet to find a solution. Every time I go for a run in the nature or even on a treadmill, I feel creative, elated and away from stress. We need to enhance running as ritual. It is just like going for a prayer to a religious place. When I run long distances, I do practice gratitude. I am always grateful that god has given me this ability to run. Many of my friends struggle to run a marathon.

I am grateful that I am surrounded with nature and peace. We often forget how lucky we are and how much we have. I just imagine if I was born in some of the difficult parts of the world or war zones like Syria, how difficult my life would have been. Probably I would have not received all the opportunities I have been given today. I would not have been able to run over 22 marathons.

Success is not always capitalising on opportunities available to us, it is also about being grateful and giving back to the world. Whenever I hear stories of any successful people like politicians, celebrities, actors, models, sports person, businessperson, I observe they all have one thing in common. They are always trying to push themselves hard to be better.

An actor plays different roles and he or she is constantly trying to be better in every role they take on. We all are actors of our lives and we need to push ourselves to greatness. Greatness cannot be achieved in a day. It needs constant hard work, discipline and consistency. No matter how much hard work we do, someone is always working harder. If I am running 50 km and boasting on the social media, someone is running 100km. If you are thinking that there is too much struggle, the fact is as long as we are alive, there is struggle. If we accept this fact our life would become a lot easier. Every day is a challenge, whether you run 50km, 100km or 1000km.

I always believe if things work its fine if it doesn't work out even better. It's a positive way of taking life not too seriously. Sometimes, we have to trust our future to destiny or karma. But that doesn't mean we should not work hard or stop trying. Sometimes, even if we are working hard and trying to achieve something, we are not able to, we still need to share this with the world to show that there is no need to feel so much pressure if things are not going the way it should be. Every good thing in the world happens with time. Bad times either destroy us or makes us strong. I experienced some really hard times when I injured my leg while running long distances. But I always recovered from any physical illness with time.

We all have dreams, big visions and unique potential to achieve great things. Nobody has come to this earth to fail but unfortunately, we all have some point in our lives. Admitting our failure makes us even stronger. We need to follow the right paths and tough times don't last but tough people do. My relationship with my family deteriorated in 2019 and I was feeling lonely and upset. I tried not to think of them, but it kept on coming into my mind. Finally, I realised I can only move forward if stop thinking of the ugly conversation, I had with them. I started meditating and it eventually helped me. I tried to focus on my energy on things I have control of. We can't do much about things we do not have control over.

Another thing is I never ran or pursued my hobby to make money. In fact, every marathon I ran I paid to charities through registration fees. So, if we are doing something only for money, we are simply wasting our time. But there is nothing wrong if we can make money doing something we love. What is important is that as long as we have some amount of money to survive, it is fine. I never felt being successful means having lots of money and possessing power and job status. But since I come from India, success is often defined in a very different way from the perspective of Indian parents.

Every Indian parent, I mean 90% of them, put lots of pressure on their children to succeed. I came from a family of doctors, engineers and civil servant. So, my father always expected me to take on one of these career paths. For them running marathon was not significant but having a job status, power and money was more important. I never felt I belonged in the family as my thinking was very different from the rest of my family.

If India loses a cricket match with Australia or Pakistan, some crazy cricket fans might burn the houses of the Indian cricketers. Just imagine how much pressure is there when 1.2 billion people want you to win the match. In a very similar manner, Indian parents also put pressure on their children to succeed. They often compare their kids with others and make them feel defeated.

There are so many Bollywood movies made to educate Indian society and change the mindset of Indian parents, but unfortunately, there is a long way to go for India to change. You can't remove the caste system which is deeply rooted in the society. Similarly, I can't change their mindset. I can't explain them that for me every profession is equally great whether you become a CEO, journalist or an actor or a doctor.

We all have the ability to do something great and it is just the matter of realisation. I realised that the best way to change their mindset is by becoming a role model. I have not been able to achieve much in my life, but I consider myself an ultra marathon runner who can write, paint, cook and have a passion for media.

Every great thing takes time and I am just looking for success like any other normal guy. But for me success means, my wellbeing and health. Running is a break from the stressful world we live in today. Stress is one of the major global problems right now. It may be due to many reasons like societal pressure, work pressure, relationship stress, financial stress due to losing a job. We all are part of it, and we can't deny that we are not facing it. But the most significant question is how we are coping with these issues.

Every time I hit the gym, I meet personal trainers, body builder with huge muscles, but when I share my running stories with them, they get surprised and tell me that they can't run even 5km. I always wonder there is no doubt they are physically strong, but are they mentally strong as well? We need people today who are mentally strong to overcome any challenges.

We all have some wisdom, strength, peace and it's up to us how we overcome challenges. Whether you are struggling to put food on the table, or you are in powerful position, we all have the ability to become the best version of ourselves. Some homeless people become drug addicts and start committing crime, while some slum dogs might try to change the world and become an inspirational millionaire.

I am so grateful in life of what I have. There are people in this planet who have no access to water, food, electricity or education. What they have is just hope. If we just Google it, we will find hundreds of such motivational stories and videos. People have become something from nothing. Reaching my goal of 70km at Shimla ultra was an achievement I always dream of. I realised that I couldn't change the world, but I can change myself by running ultra marathons.

I am planning to run some extreme races across the planet, which would help me become who I am. This passion and dream of mine needs lot of hard work, training and of course patience. But if I can inspire even one dead soul who has no hope of living life, then it's totally worth it. It has taught me important lesson that coping with bad things happening in our lives proves us how resilient we are. I am not a workaholic person, but if someone offers me a million dollars and tell me to work 16 hours a day, I would probably accept the offer for a month, in order to meet my financial needs but eventually quit in a month.

For me my wellbeing is more important than any job in the world. It may be exercise, running, healthy food and good sleep. We need all this to rejuvenate ourselves and it eventually increases our productivity at work. I read an article lately about a man in UK who runs a marathon(42km) every day before going to work. Yes, believe me or not there are some extraordinary people on this planet. I was able to connect with the article so much. What if we all start running before going to work? Will it increase our productivity? In my opinion definitely yes. Running has the ability to change our lives. We can be more happy, fruitful and focused after a run.

I found strength, happiness and fulfillment in my running

It doesn't matter whether you run 5 km or 50km, the purpose of running is to find the joy, happiness, lifestyle, love for nature and fulfillment in our lives. I am able to inspire myself by running long distances. I always think if I can run 60km than I can do anything. However, it may not be always true but running is a recipe to prepare a great dish inside our body and mind which will nourish our soul. I have never seen a sad runner. Every time I run, I see joy, happiness among runners and a feeling of great satisfaction at the finish line. I believe we all our born to run. Running is a great therapy for any kind of mental illness. It helps us recover from stress and anxiety. It's my way to refuel my body and mind to function more effectively and efficiently. We just need to find our own way of running based on individual requirements. Sometimes, I believe it is an awful tasting medicine and the patient needs it.

We live in a world today which is full of challenges. Many of my friends are facing serious life challenges. I am preparing my mind and body for the worst day of my life by running. What if I lose my job, lose my partner, family, house, what if a natural disaster strikes, what if I come to know that I have just six months to live. I would love to do everything possible which gives me joy. I will study what I love, I will find work in the field I am passionate about. I will travel, run, paint, cook, make friends and do everything which makes me feel elated. We only get to live once so there is no point of doing for long something we don't love.

When I ran 60km at the Great Ocean Road and 70km in the Himalayas, I felt so much alive and rich. I felt connected to beautiful nature. Just imagine running or cycling to work, to school and to the supermarket every day, we would be so much more active. Ultra running also teaches us the importance of time. Imagine running continuously for 12 hours.

I would always pray during the tough times for the run to pass quickly. When I am really in pain, I just pray to somehow reach the finish line. I visualise the feeling at the finish line with people cheering for me. So how much we can achieve in 12 hours is what ultra running teaches.

Running is also like a seed which grows into fruits and vegetables. Running helps our mind and body to grow, to be more creative and have a wider perspective towards life. My body and mind also adapt to long distance running, extreme temperatures and nature. Any organisation we work today has people from diverse backgrounds.

Sometimes we might not be able to adapt ourselves to new cultures, workplace environment, but running helps me to stay positive, motivated and ability to work in a team. It helps me to make the right decisions and have strong relations with my loved ones, work mates and even strangers. I grew up watching British adventurer Bear Grylls and how he adapts his body and mind to extreme environments is really commendable. I believe human body is capable of adapting to extreme challenges as well. Of course, lot of training is needed to accomplish that goal. I have different hobbies as well like painting, cooking, travelling but running is my first love.

I started running long distances just few years ago and since then have never looked back. I got to know myself better by running long distances. I have never felt the pressure to finish in a desired time but wanted to enjoy every marathon I did. I always listen to my body and every muscle and how they felt while training. When my friends on a Sunday are busy watching movies and going out for dinner, I am busy running longer distance for 8 hours by myself. I tested my limits in races running for 12 hours to 18 hours and I felt so joyful afterwards.

Running releases endorphins which makes us feel good.

Running in the mountains is extremely challenging but gives us an epic satisfaction. Without training, running in the mountains could be deadly. I have tried once in Himalayas and was able to finish 70km in nearly 13 hours. Uphill intervals help us push our limits to maximum. When it is very steep,

I usually prefer walking fast and downhill could be very easy but running too fast downhill could also lead to injury. Taking large steps and less frequent breaks, would help us achieve more. My performance in marathons originally did not improved since I started running as I never took this sport as a serious hobby. But sooner or later I started taking this hobby seriously and it is my dream to finish a marathon in around 3 hours, and also try to finish an Iron Man. Also finding time for run is very important as any long breaks between two marathons will lead to loosing stamina and fitness, and a lot of work would be needed to bring it back up.

Running taught me to test my limits and dare to take right decisions

Comfort is the thief of progress and if we are living in comfort than we can never progress. I also believe that if we are not living on the edge than we are occupying too much space. Our life is full of challenges, in fact as long as we are alive, there will be challenges. The most important thing is how we cope with these challenges.

I always believe what Steve Jobs said, 'Sometimes life will hit you in the head with a brick, don't lose faith'. We all have been hit in the head sometimes in life and it is up to us how we prepare our mind and body to recover from that injury. I started running at the age of 18 to cope with the modern challenges of the day to day life and have never stopped since.

I believe running has not only helped me become a better human being but has also helped me adapt to extreme conditions, stay motivated and become a better decision maker.

A research conducted by the Forbes had shown that one in four CEOs suffer from depression. It is very much true to say that extreme success has many strings attached and it can pull a person down completely. The point I am trying to make here is that mental health is a big issue around the world at the moment and it is costing a lot to the economy.

So how do we cope with the modern world stress, challenges and become a better leader and decision makers. I personally advocate running as a great solution to this problem. Having myself successfully completed 22 marathons in the last few years, I have learned to prepare my mind to carry out physical obstacles.

The science behind running is that interval running trains our muscles to use oxygen more efficiently. As a result, as soon as we read something after some exercise or running, we could grasp information more efficiently and effectively. Our decision-making power also gets enhanced. My first marathon was standard chartered Mumbai Marathon few years back and I finished it in 4 hours and 4 minutes. I was in pain and tired but end of the day I was glad that I did it. Later on, I started training for ultra marathons and I successfully completed 50 km Bangalore Ultra, moving on to Shimla Ultra marathon of 70km in June 2016. I ran my latest marathons in Melbourne, Sydney, Gold Coast, Great Ocean Road, Anglesea (Victoria) and it's my dream to run New York and Boston one day and test my limits.

Every time I run, I feel like I am high on something. Running is a drug to me, and I am proud to be addicted to it. I like running because exhausting myself is the most relaxing moment for me. Running has also helped me to be able to reach my goals and test my limits. When I have a goal, I stick it in my room and look at it every morning when I get up. In fact, every one of us have some kind of dreams, but very few have the courage to follow them. Many of my friends are in such a rat race that they sometimes forget to live a meaningful life. They are thinking so much about the future that they are not being able to live the present. What if I die tomorrow and will have regrets on my death bed that I was not able to follow my passion or do what I really loved. I always question myself as also my friends and family don't like me running so much.

I ask to myself is it worth my time, energy and expenses in pursuing this hobby. Am I able to make this world a better place by running? Am I able to raise awareness for the important issues of stress, mental health and anxiety? Sometimes I am successful in my runs, sometimes I am not, and it does not mean I give up on my dreams. *I know the world will love me for only one thing- for being able to do what I love.*

Trust me many people also have the ability to run or follow a passion, but they are just not aware of it. But when they see my social media post, they compare and say ok this guy is living life and maybe I am not. If I have all the money in the world, what would I do? Buy a house, car and luxury goods or I would register for marathons around the world and will travel the world by running. This would be a great experience and adventure.

Trust me no amount of money can actually make me happy as much as running and travelling the world. To appreciate what you love doing in our lives is the secret to happiness. Steve Jobs was a successful entrepreneur because he loved what he did. He was a creative genius and did what he was born to do. Just imagine if we all start doing what we are born to do, half of the world's problems will be solved. We all would be united and happier and will love our lives. Even pursuing a small hobby like painting, cooking for my friends and family gives me an epic satisfaction. Well I was inspired by other runners and I wish to motivate others to take their time off the 9 to 5 work and have time to pursue a passion or a hobby.

To choose life beyond the ordinary would eventually help us thrive in our lives. I have often come across some of my friends and family members who consider success being job status or power and money. They give lot of respect to people who possess these attributes. I personally do not consider success to that but being able to pursue your passion, have a hobby and to be able to fulfill our dreams. Today you have a job status and power, but tomorrow you might not have one.

Today you have lots of money but tomorrow, you might not have it. But one thing which will stay with us till our last breath is our passion, hobby. Sometimes when people die, they are remembered after their job status. For instance, he or she was a great journalist, doctor or actor or an athlete. These people made their passion their profession, which is great.

We excel in a certain field when we do something we love and find out what we are born to do. I was a very confused person in life. My family was always worried that I do not have a clear vision. But I eventually found that I want to have a career in Media, Film and Journalism and at the same time pursue my passion for running, painting and cooking. Sometimes, pursuing our passion takes time. But there is a saying you hang around the barber shop for long, sooner or later you will get a haircut. So, I am also currently hanging out in the hope that sooner or later I will get my break in the world of media. But I believe my passion and ability to remain hungry would eventually lead me towards my goals.

Running is the centre of my life which evolves around my love for media

I started my career as a journalist in India, but after nearly three and a half years of experience, I decided to move abroad. I was very much demotivated with the kind of journalism I was doing with the prevalence of fake news, paid news, propaganda and disinformation. It was one of the lowest paid jobs and there was clearly lack of ethics in the media.

I always believed media, film and journalism has the power to shift culture and form public opinion. Journalist have some great responsibilities but at that time in India, anyone who didn't get a job anywhere or didn't crack the civil services exam, one of the toughest exams in the world, decided to pursue a career in the Media.

There were more than 200 news channels in various languages and every channel had an official or unofficial link to a political party. I realised that this is not journalism but something else and this could lead to some serious consequences and harm the democracy.

The popularity of social media like WhatsApp and Facebook and the spread of viral fake news lead to the killings of several innocent people. Politicians often tried to spread fake rumours or news and divide the communities for their political gains.

Finally, I moved to Australia as an overseas student in 2016. I got my first media break at the Australian Broadcasting Corporation (ABC), one of the most reputable media organisation in the western world. I was an intern and used every opportunity to connect with people in this organisation. However, the corporation was going through tough times and I got to interact with the News Director of ABC, Gaven Morris and the former Managing Director, Michelle Guthrie. The ABC witnessed an $84 million funding cut from the federal government.

Then the managing director, Michelle Guthrie, was sacked and she laid charges of alleged political interference against the former chairman of the ABC, Justin Milne. I was able to raise the question of alleged political interference and the sacking of managing director at the ABC's popular talk show Q&A.

The very next day I got a text message from Michelle Guthrie saying: 'Great Question

Suki'. It was a very proud moment for me as I felt I was able to make an impact.

Few months later, I was able to raise the second question of press freedom in the Australian media after the *New York Times* described Australia as the world's most secretive democracy. The Australian Federal Police (AFP) raided the ABC and I felt Australian journalism was in a state of crisis.

When I compare the state of media in India, Australia, America and UK, I felt there is a trend of similarities around the world. If you report anything against the government, there are chances of prosecution in countries where there is no democracy.

I heard a joke on the internet that someone said about Australia, as far as press freedom is concerned be better than North Korea. I did feel that journalism is not a crime but is definitely in a state of crisis.

I did work at Monash University as a research assistant and at Coles supermarket, to be able to pay my bills, but I wish to change the trends in the media as I have a passion for it. Running has taught me to stay positive and follow my passion.

I know very well how hard it is to get a break in the western media, especially being a person of colour, but everything is possible, if we are persistent and have the ability to work hard.

When I was interning at the ABC, I was so grateful to have an amazing supervisor, Vipul Khosla and another mentor Dr. Prashath Pillay. They were so nice to me that I cooked some curries and brought some cake for them on my last day. I was also employed there for a while to analyse the diversity content of the ABC.

I also got to meet some of my favourite Australian TV presenters Michael Rowland and Virginia Trioli. I was bit nervous, but I took the courage to meet them behind the studio of the News Breakfast, Australia's popular morning news show. I told them all the good things about the ABC and how diversity is represented well and how the public broadcaster is different from the commercial channels.

Finally, I walked out of the ABC on June 15, 2018, my official last day. I do often visit as an audience member at the Q&A program as I believe the show has an ability to create an impact. They raise several issues happening in Australia and around the world and I have often met the former producer of this program Peter McEnvoy, who always have a lovely smile on his face. I did visit a public event at the SBS, another public broadcaster in Australia, at their audience-based event. I connected with some great journalist from Indigenous and British background.

I do often attend events and conferences on media as it helps me remain updated to the latest developments and trends in the media. But I am very much sure someday I will get another break in the media. Meanwhile, I started running even more when I was getting rejections from my job applications.

I thought running might help me recover from the stress and anxiety, I was facing. Whatever money I earn, I spend on running long distances. Running has now become the centre of my life, but that doesn't mean I have given up my passion for media after several rejections. Rejections are just redirection and sometimes, even if we work really hard, we can still face failure, so we need to have patience. There is always a time for everything and so no point of taking too much stress.

During this period of uncertainty in my life, I decided to pursue my passions. Steve Jobs said, 'if today is the last day of your life, are going to do what you are about to do today'. I finally got the answer. I decided to do everything which would help me feel good. I decided to run marathons and aimed to finish in around 3 hours.

I decided to maintain healthy relationship with my friends, to travel a bit, and cook a healthy meal once a week. Trust me job hunting is a difficult job and it is even more difficult in my field of journalism.

I decided to write my blogs on a more regular basis, it eventually helped me in improving my writing skills. Finally, I decided to write a book on running. Running is not my profession but my passion. But what if my passion eventually leads me to my career in media. I felt many people want a job so that they can pay their bills, but when there is a serious job crisis, people are willing to take any job in order to survive.

We all have to do something to survive but yes getting dream job takes time. So, I put my focus towards running for a while. I thought why not focus on my health, diet and sleep instead of taking on so much stress of getting a dream job.

Indian parents put lot of pressure on their children to succeed and especially when their children go abroad to study, the expectations are very high. My father was very disappointed with me, he never appreciated my passion for media, running and other hobbies. He just wanted me to have a decent job and get married with a girl of his choice so that he can boast around the village about my success. My brother and his wife unfortunately were also not supportive.

I always knew, I was born to do something special. My vision was very different from my family. I was observing the world from a very different angle than my family. I knew it I was born to create an impact. In fact, I was already able to create an impact by my questions at the ABC's Q&A. I wish to also create an impact with my runs someday.

Earlier in 2019, I met Australian Marathon runner Mina Guli. She ran 60 marathons in 60 days around the world to raise awareness of water crisis. When I asked her why water, she explained me about the difficulties of living without water in some of the difficult parts of the world. She informed me everything is made from water and if we start conserving water we would be able to save lives. I connected with her so much that I thought of starting my own campaign on raising the issue of mental health. Mental health is a very big issue in Australia and one in four people in this country is suffering from stress, anxiety and depression. I gained some wisdom by running when I myself was suffering from a serious anxiety attack in April 2019. I thought of being so much grateful of the opportunities I had and decided to practice gratitude every morning instead of complaining. It eventually helped me stay happy.

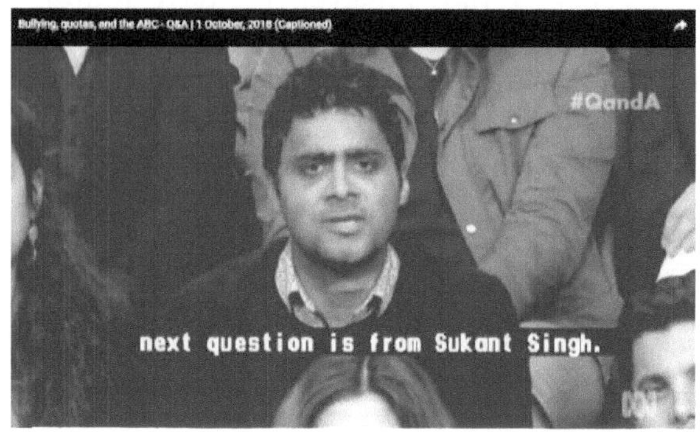

I appeared on popular talk show Q&A for the second time, raising an important issue of alleged political interference at the ABC and freedom of press in Australia.

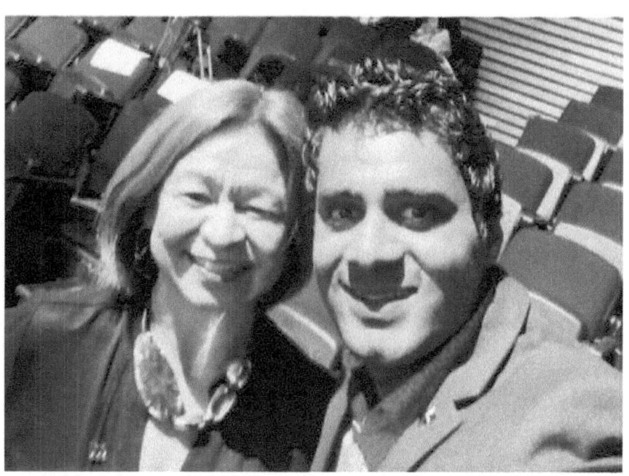

With former ABC Managing Director, Michelle Guthrie. One of the sweetest person, I met at the ABC.

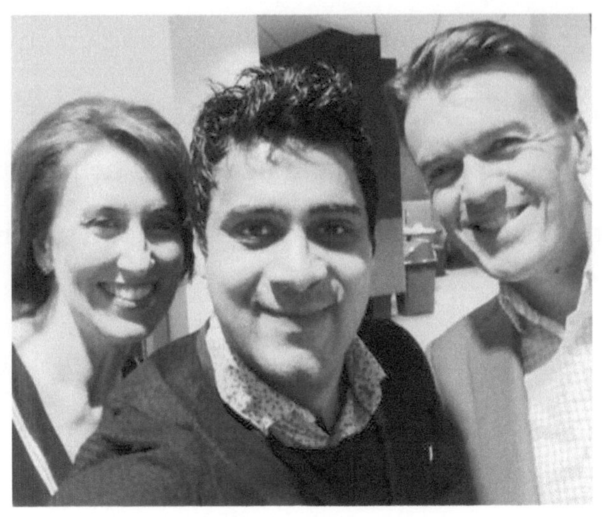

With ABC presenters Virginia Trioli and Michael Rowland. I met them on the last day as an intern at the Australian Broadcasting Corporation

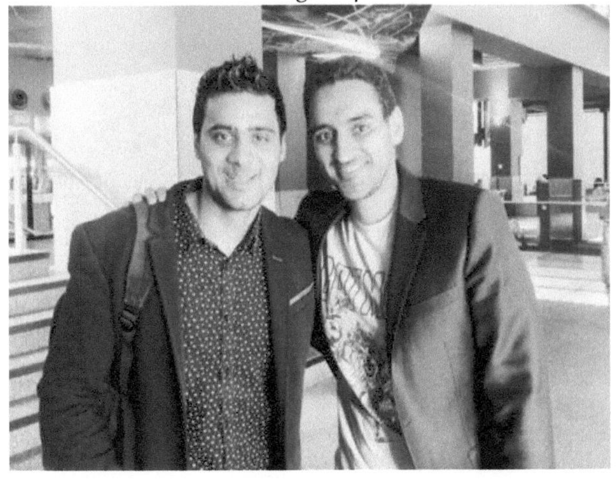

With Australian Broadcaster and my former lecturer at Monash university, Waleed Aly

Running also taught me about being creative, genuine, confident, helped me develop leadership qualities and eventually helped me in decision making. Everything I do in my life I compare it to running.

If I can run 100km, anything is possible. For me taking care of my mental and physical health is as important as my passion for media, film and journalism. I very well know I can enhance my performance at work if I go for a run every morning or cycling, swimming.

As an athlete, I try to focus in preparing myself mentally and physically. Mindfulness and meditation are like doing reps in the gym and it also help me to focus well and help me improve my listening skills. Every time before a big race, I try to visualise and focus on my goals. Just imagine if all the journalist, media personalities and people in the film industries like actors, comedians, producers start practicing mindfulness and start running marathons. There is no doubt their performance would be enhanced at work.

I very well know journalist go through lot of hardships in their profession. They often come across some very disturbing stories, which might impact their mental health. Also, the work pressure in the newsroom is very high. People are expected to finish a story within a deadline.

I remember covering the Nirbhaya Gang rape incident in 2012 in New Delhi for NDTV and it was one of the most disturbing stories I covered. The incident brought a movement of revolution regarding safety of women in India. Finally, a documentary was made on this brutal gang rape and murder, called India's daughter by a British film maker. This story was so disturbing, and observing the massive protest for days across India, I felt very much ashamed as an Indian and as a journalist. I went for a run and worked out in the gym to feel better.

Likewise, I can very well imagine journalist working in some of the difficult parts of the world like Syria, Afghanistan, Kashmir, China. It is full of challenges and if one reports against the government, a journalist might face prosecution.

There are several media literacy programs also being held to educate the journalists and help them recover from any stress and trauma. The job of an investigative journalist is even more challenging. I truly believe that Australia is a bit less corrupt today than other developed nations because of Four Corners. It is one of my favourite show at the ABC which reveals various scams, and it is an effort to fight corruption. The root cause of global problems like poverty, inequality, terrorism is nothing but corruption. Corruption leads to other basic problems in our society. Four Corners has had a huge impact in Australian society by being able to fight corruption for decades.

What I am trying to share is that if all investigative journalist or people from any profession start running marathons with me, they would love their job even more. What if our horrible bosses also start running marathons, he or she won't be horrible anymore.

Getting enough sleep is also important along with physical exercise. Our body needs 8 hours of sleep, which helps us to recharge our mental and emotional health. Running, Yoga, meditation, cycling, swimming is not just tools to enhance my performance, but they have become a way to live life. Yes, many journalists have a busy life and they have to travel around the world to cover stories. But taking time for 45 minutes for our health everyday could enhance our wellbeing and performance.

Using the platform of media, I wish to create a positive impact in the world but at the same time I wish to create awareness that taking care of ourselves, leading a balanced lives, being healthy, eating right, having healthy relationships is as important as our work as a journalist.

Since I moved to Australia in 2016, I was not able to make a single friend from my home country, India. I felt very strange as everyone was in a rat race to make lots of money, get permanent residency, citizenship, get their dream job, buy a house, car and then go back to third world countries and boast about their success. I felt I was so different. I was not chasing that so called 'success'. The definition of success according to me was completely different than my friends. I believed in following in my passion and my dreams. Running is my passion and media is my dream.

If I am able to accomplish both these things, I would be the happiest person in the world. Trust me no amount of money can give me joy as much as I get at the finish line of every marathon. I feel like I am alive and being able to live a meaningful life, as most of my friends are not being able to as they are in a rat race.

I know millions of people including some of my family members who equate success with money and job status/power. One of my uncles who is a civil servant in India gets VIP treatment wherever he goes, and one of my uncles who is farmer gets very poor treatment without any respect. The good thing I like about Australia is that whether you are a cleaner or a CEO you get equal treatment in society. I always believe, we should not judge somebody by the colour of their skin or by their job status. But unfortunately, the society I come from, people judge you by your job status.

I ask to myself sometimes, what if I win a million-dollar lottery tomorrow. What will I do with that much of money? Will it change my life? I would absolutely say no. I will be the same person and I would use that money to travel the world and run marathons for various causes and change the lives of people who are really in need. I am so grateful for all the opportunities I got in life but there are several people around the world who are dying every day without food and water, living in extreme poverty. I have come across people in Australia who are desperately looking for promotion, a million-dollar lottery ticket and a better life but I realised, even though you have all the basic facilities, people are still not happy. There is lack of fulfillment in their lives.

One in four people suffer from anxiety, stress, depression. Probably people living in third world countries are much happier. What is possibly going wrong? What I am trying to say is that we all need a hobby and a break from money, power, job status once a week at least. For me it is running, for you it could be anything from travelling to playing a musical instrument.

On August 25, 2019, I again ran a 60km ultra marathon all by myself. I realised running a marathon is easy but running long distances all by yourself is tough. In marathons there are so many other runners who motivate you, volunteers offer you food and drinks and spectators cheer for you in all the tracks. It makes it a lot easier to run long distances when you have a support crew and people all around. But when I am running all by myself such a distance like 60km, I need self-discipline. I keep motivating myself and when I am really tired, and I try to find a random stranger and tell him or her of my running story.

Most of the strangers motivate me and I feel good about it. Trust me I ran the same distance in a much more difficult track in exactly 6 hours and 30 minutes two months ago. And this time I finished in 9 hours. It is only because I was running alone. Similarly, the importance of working together and in a great team always enhances our efficiency.

Teamwork is such an important skill which probably every organisation in the world needs right now. And running marathons have made me realise the importance of leadership and teamwork.

Just imagine if we give ourselves one day to refuel ourselves, to pursue a hobby. Passion is very important and trust me no amount of money can give me epic satisfaction as much as I get at the finish line of a marathon. Yes, it is important to make money and there is nothing wrong in having a job status.

Everyone one of us have to work hard to pay our bills but we definitely need to take time to take care of our health. Eating a healthy diet and physical exercise should be part of our lives. I live in a country where every one of my friends is in a rat race to make lots and lots of money. My friends love boasting on social media about their new job status, marriage status, new house, new car, new citizenship status of their desired country and I love boasting about the power of my legs on social media. But I am saying nobody cares for your new job status and whether you got married or divorced.

What I care about is that on average more than 2 people per day commit suicide in Australia and it never gets reported in the media. As the *New York Times* called it once, it is one of the world's most secretive democracy. The world is not aware what is happening in this island nation. When I was running 60km all by myself, I came across a car wash place, which also had a dog wash facility. I closely watched people washing their dogs along with their cars. It was a funny moment for me as I felt they love dogs so much in this country. There are dog police, veterinary doctors and if you get to visit a supermarket in Australia, there is a separate aisle for dogs. There are 100 varieties of dog foods, dog clothes, dog bed and dog party mix. There is nothing wrong in loving dogs so much, but I am asking one simple question, have we lost faith in humanity.

There is a homeless man sleeping in the streets on a cold winter night at flinders street in Melbourne and nobody gives a damn. He or she has probably not taken a shower in six months so why there is no facility to wash homeless people in this country as well. We all are born to love and embrace humanity. Loving dogs is as important as loving humans.

We all are dealing with some kind of stress and anxiety, as sometimes life can be daunting. If we all start running marathons, the world would be a better place full of healthy, productive people. I love running as much as I love media. Healthy media is an essential pillar of a functioning democracy and I do get disappointed sometimes when I see biased reporting or fake news content going viral. Despite media's imperfections, it is an essential pillar of a healthy democracy.

Unfortunately, the public broadcaster like the ABC have experienced several funding cuts in the past few years again and again. Some of the best and the brightest journalist have been shown the door. ABC is one of the most prestigious institution in Australia and politicians have repeatedly tried to punish this institution by funding cuts and police raids and alleged political interference.

I was also disappointed by the government and the media for not being able to reconcile indigenous and non-indigenous Australians. Indigenous people have lived in this land for over 60,000 years and shockingly they were not even counted in the census for a very long time. Even today the suicide rates among indigenous Australians are very high. They have lost their land, identity and somehow, they feel like they don't belong in their own land.

Unfortunately, it never gets reported in the front page of the newspapers. I felt somehow media has a great responsibility to embrace diversity and be unbiased in its reporting. It has the power to educate people and make an impact. A biased media could result in detrimental consequences in the society and may lead to further division among communities.

Running has also taught me to be more productive and love my work. I wish one day to be able to set the standard of media houses really high so that there is no place for disinformation, fake news and propaganda. Running marathons and my love for media also reminds me of the BBC news presenter Sophie Raworth, who completed 150-mile desert ultra marathon, called Marathon Des Sables in the Sahara Desert.

She crossed the finish lines with her friends, and the runners in these extreme marathons had to take no shower for nine days and live in a tent along with other runners. Every day after running for five to six hours, runners returned to their tents. I can only imagine surviving for nine days in the heat when you sweat so much without shower and proper toilet would be very challenging. Runners were given a brown paper plastic bag with plastic cubicle to relieve themselves. It would have been one hell of an experience.

It is said that when we are lying on our death bed, people will always forget how much money they made but will always cherish their life experiences. And we need to encourage these life experiences, which will stay with us forever and also teach us to live in extreme conditions.

Every time I cross the finish line, I actually couldn't believe I have done it. Running ultra marathons have taught me that my body is so much stronger than my mind ever believed. I could relate myself so much to running and media because both have the ability to give back to the society we live in today. We all are programmed for generosity and when I am running marathons, I am grateful for all the opportunities I got, and I am volunteering to give back to the people in need. Every marathon I ran, I have been able to raise money through various charities and I have realised that the purpose of my life is to give, love, care, practice empathy and compassion.

We are living in a world today where there is multiple economic, environmental and social crisis and we can't depend on the government and god to save us. There is a serious climate crisis around the world and global warming is leading to various other problems. I am trying to say is that if we all start taking one global issue and start running and uniting the world, half of the world's problems could be solved.

We all have the ability to become leaders and save this world from multiple crisis. I am just asking what if God is also dependent on us. When many of my friends are enjoying their weekend with movies and dinner, I am running long distances. By running I am volunteering to save lives, raise awareness of mental health issues and making a difference in the lives of millions of people who have given up on their lives.

There is no doubt that we all are born to give and not just take. Giving send a message to universe that we all have what we need. The Bible and the Bhagavad Gita talks in deep about generosity. The Bible says, '**we will be judged by the things we do the least among us**'. While the Bhagavad Gita says that through '**selfless sacrifice, one will always be fruitful and find fulfillment of our desires'**. It also talks about a life which is full of greed and success if defined by making lots of money. But to be honest there is no limits to possessing wealth. We can have all the money in the world, but there will be always be some lack of fulfillment unless we start giving back to the world and serve the humanity. I love what Dalai Lama said, '**our prime purpose in life is to help others and if you can't help them at least don't hurt them**'.

Every time I run marathons, I feel like humanity is the most beautiful thing on earth. Yes, we do lose faith in humanity after having some bitter experiences, but that doesn't mean the world is only full of toxic people. Many of my friends are in a rat race to make lots and lots of money. They are making so much money that they don't even have time to spend. They have no time to take care of their health or get a proper 8 hours sleep. Dalai Lama beautifully says about humanity and what surprises him the most is that, 'Man sacrifices his health in order to make money. Then he sacrifices money to recuperate his health, and then he is so anxious about the future that he does not enjoy the present, as a result he is not able to live in the present or the future, he lives as he is never going to die, then dies having never really lived'.

They are worrying so much about the future that they forget to enjoy the present. What if we die tomorrow? Are we going to regret that we didn't follow a passion or a hobby? We didn't pursue a career that we wanted to do as we were so much trapped by other people's thinking. We all need to embrace generosity for a better world. Whenever there is a natural disaster or economic slowdown, we have seen people coming over from all corners of the world to help. We need world leaders today who unite the world and not divide it. When New Zealand witnessed terror in early 2019, the entire population of the island nation got united. And the Prime Minister Jacinda Ardern became a role model PM around the world, who united the country by wearing a burqa and sent a deep message that there is no place for hatred in her country.

In fact, we don't have to wait for a natural disaster or such massacre to show compassion and generosity, but every day we are surrounded by opportunities to act on the same instinct of giving and helping others. In fact, we are so wired for generosity that our genes reward us when we give and punish us when we don't. Many researches at some of the greatest universities in the world have proved that when we volunteer our life expectancy increases. When I see young kids and old people volunteering at the marathons, I feel they are not only doing a great job but also giving back. It also helps them live a meaningful life. When we volunteer, we don't get paid for it. It is a selfless sacrifice we are doing to help the humanity.

Similarly, as an aspiring journalist in Australia and a former journalist in India, I feel I have a great obligation to tell stories of people in need. Media has the power to tell the stories of people in need and create an impact and change lives.

There is no place for corruption in the media and any unethical practices. As a responsible media houses, journalist should not be biased in reporting and give a true picture to the world. Mindfulness and media literacy programs are highly encouraged to help journalist do their job properly. Some of them often come across very disturbing stories, which could impact their mental wellbeing. I often advocate running marathons for every journalist, as it could help them enhance their performance as well their professional and personal relationships.

I do recommend practicing getting proper sleep after and before a run. It would eventually help us improve our health, creativity and productivity.

I am a fitness freak and going to gym is another hobby, which makes me feel good about myself. Focusing on our breathing while meditating once a day also relieves us from any stress and anxiety. Today yoga, which originated in India, has gained more popularity in the west because life is more stressful in the west than ever. Today you have a job, probably tomorrow you won't have one. Today you have a partner or family, tomorrow they might not be there. So how do we cope with these challenges. I personally advocate running as one of the best solutions to cope with the modern-day stress. Apart from running, meditation, even a long walk in nature, exercise, yoga and reconnecting with our loved ones has the ability to enhance our level of happiness.

Many people are able to feel better surrounded by their pets. It also impacts their health and happiness. But I personally don't feel great surrounded by pets, but doing what I love, helps me feel good about myself. It could be going for a run, painting, cooking and of course following news and media. Walking, running, cycling, gardening help protect us from mental health issues.

In Australia, one of my favourite show is ABC's Q&A and when I was watching one day, I was appalled to hear that one in four Victorians are suffering from anxiety, stress due to their relationships, career and health issues. Suicide rates among young males and indigenous youths are predominantly high. I realised there is something seriously going wrong where everyone's priority is to achieve success, and success according to them is defined as money and power/ job status. Everyone has come to this land in search of gold.

Nobody wants to be poor and a failure. But in search of money and power, are we losing something more precious like our relationships. Are we losing our peace of mind, human connections and love? Sadly, I was not able to make a single friend from my country, India in a foreign land as everyone was in a rat race to become wealthier and achieve the height of success. But in terms of my favourite author Arianna Huffington, that kind of success, is a two-legged stool and sooner or later you will fall off.

Today, when the rate of depression and mental illness is so high, we need more marathon runners, we need more stronger relationships and human connections. According to World Health Organization, more than 350 million people around the world are suffering from depression.

There could be many factors behind that-our lifestyle, sleep pattern, work pressure, relationships. Our work performance enhances if we focus on our sleep, exercise, diet and of course relationships. No amount of money and job status can give me the happiness I have when I reach the finish line of a marathon. I am the happiest person in the world after being able to finish a marathon and ultra marathon. Today most of the companies want to recruit people whose priority is to focus on their mental and physical fitness. A healthy person is more likely to me more productive than an unhealthy person.

Some big tech companies like Google, Microsoft, Apple, Facebook focuses on the wellness and mental wellbeing of their employees. If we are not getting proper sleep, our decision-making ability, creativity and performance could be affected.

When I run marathons, I often come across CEOs and people who have a very stressful and busy lifestyle. They run marathons to definitely enhance their performance and release the pressure of work they are going through. I personally don't run to win races or to go places, but I run to escape, to find peace and be free. I am just being myself when I am running, and I also come across like-minded people like myself. I attract myself towards positive people and I feel like I am trying to get away from toxic and negative people.

Every day one small act of kindness like helping a disabled person cross the road, being kind to people we take for granted, like the barista who makes a wonderful coffee and building some kind of human connection could actually enhance our wellbeing and the entire day we will be in a happy state.

When I work in customer service, I try to make best human connection possible with the customers. Making eye contact, smiling and greeting them was a skill I learnt while doing an assignment on Walmart in University. I used this skill to make human connections and telling the customers a story behind the product. This is a unique skill which could enhance our output. And when I come across horrible abusive customers, I still smiled. Some people might provoke you but we just need to remain calm and not give much importance to unacceptable behaviour.

During marathons, I have also seen one runner helping another and a small act of kindness during marathon can inspire millions of people to do the same. The aftermath of the bombing in Boston Marathon in 2013, saw an act of human kindness displayed by people from all walks of life who did whatever they could to save lives. Many marathon runners after finishing the race rushed to hospital to donate blood to victims. Such act of human kindness reflect how we are wired for generosity. We should not act like that only during disasters and tragedies but in our everyday lives.

Running has taught me to live life in a meaningful way, but I do have other hobbies as well which helps me become the best version of myself. I love painting as well.

How Art Therapy helped me de-stress

Painting a canvas is like a meditation to me. I go all the way into a different world when I lock myself in a room and test my creativity. I usually love making portraits as it encourages my creativity and I am able to express myself. It eventually helps me de-stress, improve self-esteem and build my confidence. When you create something out of nothing, it's a great feeling.

Imagine going to a networking event and giving the portrait made by you to the person whom you consider as a role model. It would really give a great impression. We have the ability to paint but just some of us are lazy enough to try this hobby. Just imagine, when we were a child, all of us painted. But as we grow up, our hobbies eventually fade away.

We don't have to be a professional painter to communicate our thoughts. I started first by sketching, using charcoal on canvas, then I moved to acrylic on canvas. It adds lots of creativeness to my imaginative thinking and help my mind relax. I am able to communicate with the world through my paintings. For me making a portrait first with a pencil is a difficult job but once I finish creating the outline, I love playing with colours over it. I try to take care of shades and put mix of colours gently.

I remember winning the first prize when I was in primary school for painting. My name was in the newspaper the next day and my parents were really proud of me. I didn't continue painting for a long time, but I did choose fine arts in school in my 12th grade. I remember, I was the only boy in the class, and it was bit embarrassing for me. I guess painting was more a girl thing that time.

Boys were more into sports, but I loved painting. I scored above 90% in fine arts and was really proud of that. But as it is said, art does not pay the bills so making a career as an artist is really difficult. But there is nothing wrong in having it as a hobby. It has great benefits and helps us de-stress and become more creative.

I remember selling some of my paintings in the Himalayas. One of the them I sold was the portrait of Mahatma Gandhi for Aud$100. I also donated some of my sketches to charity organizations like Paint our World. Recently I founded Suki's art.online, an organisation which focuses on raising money for the indigenous people of the world. Art has helped people with life threatening illness, and I am just trying to spread the message that just like running, painting also helps us recover from various kinds of illness. There are so many diseases in the world which might not have a cure, but certain therapies have the ability to make our life better.

Harvard Medical School research proved that creating visual art reduces stress and promotes relaxation in people who are hospitalised due to illness. Art has also proved to be huge beneficial to people suffering from dementia. Art is a way to express ourselves when we are alone and achieve a sense of fulfillment. Research has found that when people express themselves through art it can help them recover from depression, anxiety and even severe diseases like cancer.

I also love painting natural landscapes. It helps me connect with nature. I imagine the beauty of nature and try to express it in my art. I am not a professional artist. But some people motivate me while some criticise, but I love the feeling of creating something colourful.

I do recommend just start doing some kind of painting for one hour every week and see the difference. If we don't have a hobby trust me, we are not living life. I try to paint sometimes, in order to refuel myself. Art encourages us sometimes to keep fighting as life is not easy sometimes.

I have seen children suffering from autism and being able to communicate through art. Children with any kind of disability are been able to communicate through art and music. I do not play any musical instrument, but music and art are both therapeutic medicines. Playing a musical instrument also enhances our focus and listening ability. I Wish I could play a musical instrument.

Recently, I also did a course on Improv Comedy in Melbourne. I got a diversity scholarship to pursue this 8-week program. Some great lessons I learnt was teamwork and focusing on listening.

This is a Chicago style comedy which is not scripted, and one has to create a story from a word given by the audience. I had no idea I could make people laugh. I did perform after the 8-week course, but it was one of the most challenging things I did. I was completely out of my comfort zone. We were taught to establish base reality-who, what, where. The audience should be able to understand in 30 seconds, what we were doing, where are we and what role we are playing. I also learnt how to perform under pressure and support each other in building the role further. Improv comedy teaches us various life skills and I do recommend it to people from all corners of life. It is also a therapeutic medicine just like painting, running. The ability to make somebody laugh is the best feeling. We are already living in a stressful world where people often forget how to laugh. Laughter is the best medicine and Improv taught me to laugh and to make people laugh.

My friends told me you are the only one who can cook and run at the same time

I can cook more than 20 curries. Yes, I am not lying. It is a skill I developed since my mom taught me at a young age. Cooking is a stress reliever as well and a healthy choice. We often rely on eating in restaurants in the western world but cooking at home is always a great choice. Over the last three years in Australia, I have been able to cook various curries for my friends. I love cooking for others more than myself. I feel there is a way to build human connection by cooking. My friends love my curries. At work I am able to build relations by cooking.

My favourite dishes are biryani, butter chicken, egg curry, fish salad, potato fries, dal, lady fingers, French toast, chicken curry, dosa. Most of these are Indian curries which is not very healthy but is good once a while to have those. Most of the Indian curries have similar spices so it is actually not a difficult job to cook.

I believe all of us can cook. Just because we haven't tried that does not mean we can't cook. Many of us are lazy or we give ourselves the bad excuse that we don't have time to cook but we don't have to be a master chef to cook. We just need some patience and enthusiasm. It is definitely cheaper to cook at home than to eat outside. Cooking for our loved ones also enhances our relationships. I often have experienced an honest conversation with work mates or my friends after inviting them for dinner.

Cooking is also an art. Just like we play with colour, we need to play with spices and vegetables in order to cook a dish. When we cook, we do physical work which helps us break us the 9 to 5 circle and overcome mental exhaustion. I feel more serene and relaxed. Even just baking cakes help improve our individual mindset. If we try making a new dish, it also boosts our confidence once the dish is completed. Cooking is also proved to be therapeutic in dealing with stress, anxiety. It is a great way to motivate people to come together and socialise. Indian food is popular around the world and I have been able to build human connections by being able to cook various curries.

But to be honest there is no connection between my cooking and running skills. I believe I am a creative person and there is a deep connection in my paintings, running habits and my cooking skills. I am trying to be able to connect the dots by embracing these skills in my life. These hobbies affect my mind, emotions and body. I also try to help someone who could benefit from my skills.

These skills have made me realise that the objective of my life is to create an impact, to serve the humanity. I often try to be a giver rather than taker and reconnect myself to the world and the nature. Through running, painting, cooking I am not only able to connect the dots but able to share my journey to be able to deal with life challenges.

I am able to help people who are going through lot of stress by sharing my message that no amount of joy, money and power can give me as much self-satisfaction as what I get at the finish line of a marathon. Making money is important to survive but should not be our primary goal. We need to pursue our hobbies, connect with humans and take care of our wellbeing. And as Mahatama Gandhi said, '**In a gentle way you can shake the world**'.

We don't have to be violent to create an impact. Sometimes mere words of wisdom, a piece of writing and a peaceful message could prevent a war. We all have the ability to create an impact and we can do it by doing what we love. An artist can create an impact with his or her paintings. A runner can inspire people to be fit and healthy. I love another quote from Mahatma Gandhi. He said, **'You never know what results come of your actions, but if you do nothing there will be no results**.' Every time I fail, at least I try. Trust me many people don't even try running a marathon or painting or cooking.

You don't have to be a Leonardo Da Vinci in order to paint. Just play with some colours and eventually you will end up creating something. Trust me many people will not even try painting thinking they are bad at it.

But nobody is a born artist. Yes, some people are gifted but most of the successful people have become successful after repeated failures in their lives. When I run, I do not want to be Usain Bolt. I just want to run because it makes me feel good about myself and I enjoy it. But if I keep running marathons, someday I do have a possibility of even winning a marathon. Just running a marathon is very big deal and accomplishment for many.

Forget about winning. But at least I am trying and not have the negative mindset and that only elite athletes can win marathons. If we train hard, we definitely have the ability to achieve success.

By following these rules I am just trying to lose myself in the service of humanity. The goal of my life is not to make billions of dollars but to serve humanity, to help people change their lives, inspire people to run and cure their mental illness. When I run marathons or pursue a hobby I am actually volunteering for my happiness and happiness of others. It eventually makes me healthier, in better mood and overcome stress. It gives me a purpose to life and strengthen my immune system. It enhances my time management skills and helps me connect with peers. I did laugh when one of my friends told me once that you are only one who can cook and run at the same time. Yes, I love both the hobbies and when I overeat on curries, I try to burn calories while running. The most important thing is it helps me connect with mates and make meaningful connections with my family, friends, loved ones and even strangers.

Acknowledgments

Writing this book was a dream and I am so grateful; dreams do come true. I have been working on this book for the last six months and use to sneak into the local Monash Library in Clayton, Victoria to write. I am so grateful to the Library for the support. Since this book is on my passion for running, I would like to thank some extraordinary people I met in various marathons like Sydney Marathon, Surf Coast Century, Great Ocean Road Marathon. Also, I would have not been alive today if I didn't have my amazing support crew Hui and Nancy who were tracking me through the race map app when I got lost, during the Surf Coast Century challenge. I need to thank some special people

I met in Australia; Caron Dann, my former supervisor and lecturer at Monash University, who gave me an amazing letter of recommendation and always motivated me to follow my passion for running and media. I also want to thank my editor Blaise van Hecke for her kindness, support and some great advice on this book.

Special thanks to some leaders I met at the Australian Broadcasting Corporation, Gaven Morris, Michelle Guthrie, Michael Rowland, Virginia Trioli, Waleed Aly, Vipul Khosla, Prashanth Pillay, whom I consider as role models in the media industry. And finally, I dedicate this book to the woman I loved the most in my life, my mum who passed away nearly 18 years ago.

Resources

- According to a journal by *Science Daily,* "Science has proved that one of the major reasons for anxiety and depression is the wrong kind of foods like fast food we are eating today": https://www.sciencedaily.com/releases/2012/03/120330081352.htm

- According to *WHO,* every 40 seconds someone commits suicide due to mental illness. This is an official 2018 data from World Health Organisation: https://www.who.int/mental_health/prevention/suicide/suicideprevent/en/

- Forbes research says, "one in four CEOs are suffering from depression": https://www.forbes.com/sites/cherylsnappconn

er/2013/05/14/how-mental-illness-makes-some-executives-stronger/#4afe8ee94c5d

- "The Shark Experiment" mentioned in the book is based on the article from Elite Readers by Kathrina: https://www.elitereaders.com/shark-experiment-story-breaks-through-mental-barriers-motivation/

www.ingramcontent.com/pod-product-compliance
Ingram Content Group UK Ltd.
Pitfield, Milton Keynes, MK11 3LW, UK
UKHW040004200726
13854UKWH00001B/36

9 780648 715306